Crime free housing

Crime free housing

Barry Poyner and Barry Webb

Butterworth-Architecture

Butterworth Architecture
An imprint of Butterworth-Heinemann Ltd
Linacre House, Jordan Hill, Oxford OX2 8DP

 PART OF REED INTERNATIONAL BOOKS

OXFORD   LONDON   BOSTON
MUNICH   NEW DELHI   SINGAPORE   SYDNEY
TOKYO   TORONTO   WELLINGTON

First published 1991

British Library Cataloguing in Publication Data
A catalogue record for this book is available from the British Library

Library of Congress Cataloguing in Publication Data
A catalogue record for this book is available from the Library of Congress

ISBN 0 7506 1273 8

Photoset by Genesis Typesetting, Laser Quay, Rochester, Kent
Printed and bound by M & A Thomson Litho Ltd., East Kilbride, Scotland

Foreword

This book sets out to investigate some of the fundamental questions associated with crime and dwellings which until now have either not been researched or only partly so.

The statistics associated with crime and dwellings currently available have either been generalized to such an extent as to be of little use or categorized by various agencies in an arbitrary way. Thus, information from which the real causes of crime or its solution might be determined is not available. The authors have set about the task of trying to identify the reasons for crime and to make recommendations on how it can be 'designed out' wherever possible. In doing so, some of the myths which have formed the basis of previous works are exposed. In other cases the authors have confirmed previous theories from their detailed research.

It was fortuitous that Barry Poyner was a member of the working party which produced *NHBC Guidance on how the Security of New Homes can be Improved*. As Chairman of the working party, I know that with his help and knowledge of the subject many lengthy discussions were avoided. The working party also had confidence in the recommendations which it made. In addition to the *Guidance* document, NHBC have incorporated into its requirements those aspects which are under the builder's control such as locks on doors and windows. These have been applied to all new houses since January 1989.

This book now sets out to show that by careful thought during the design and layout stage, crime free housing is a possibility. Builders and architects will find the conclusions, in a checklist format, of great assistance in planning new projects, not least as the reasons for the recommendations are given.

This book will be of benefit to all involved in the design of housing.

Graham Pye
1990 President
The House Builders' Federation

Acknowledgements

This book would not have been possible without financial support from Sir Clifford Chetwood, Chairman and Chief Executive of George Wimpey PLC, from the Housing Research Foundation and from Mr and Mrs J. A. Pye's Charitable Settlement. Thanks are also due to Graham Pye for his help and encouragement. Funding for the earlier research on crime and housing layout was provided by a grant from the Home Office.

The authors would like to thank the Metropolitan Police for allowing them access to crime reports for Harrow, and the Chief Constable of Northamptonshire for providing crime data during both stages of the research study.

Contents

Summary of design requirements

Moderate locking security. Houses require only a moderate level of locking security, provided the opportunity for crime is controlled by the design and layout of a housing area.

Facing windows. The front windows of houses should face each other across the street or similar shared access area, to create a system of mutual surveillance.

High fences at the sides and rear. The side and rear boundaries of individual house plots should be provided with full-height fencing or walls.

Front access to a secure yard. There should be a gateway at the front of the house giving access to a secure yard or garden area. This gateway should be designed so that it can be locked or bolted on the inside and supervised from inside the house.

Access for servicing and deliveries. There should be a place to store waste bins and provide access to gas and electricity meters at the front of the house. It is also desirable to provide a place by the front door where deliveries can be left under cover and out of sight of the public footpath.

Space at the front. There seems to be a need for an area in front of the house between the house and public access areas.

On-curtilage hardstanding for cars. All car parking should be on hardstandings within the curtilage of the house, preferably at the front to facilitate surveillance.

A garage at the side of the house. Any garage should be provided at the side of the house, close to the front entrance.

Limit road access. It is an advantage to reduce the number of road access points to an area of housing and so avoid creating through traffic routes.

Avoid through pedestrian routes. Where pedestrian routes are separate from the roadways, they should not be planned to create a series of through routes connecting with other housing areas or open spaces.

Surveillance of access roads. Houses should be oriented to face access routes and especially to focus on points of entry into an area to provide intensive surveillance.

Green spaces outside housing areas. Green open spaces should be provided near the entrances to housing areas rather than within them.

1 Introduction

[handwritten annotation: look up differences between america & canada gun laws — illustrate - same laws different outcomes]

From the mid-1950s official statistics show an unprecedented growth of crime in Britain. In thirty years the rate of officially reported crime in England and Wales increased eightfold, from just under 1000 offences per 100 000 population to nearly 8000 (Home Office, 1988). Similar patterns can be found in other countries such as the United States and Canada. Although it is uncertain how accurately official statistics represent changes in criminal behaviour, few doubt that a major increase in crime has occurred. Crime has become a serious social problem.

Residential neighbourhoods do not escape from crime. Much of the concern about the failure of public sector housing, particularly the medium- and high-rise housing of the 1960s and early 1970s, has focused on crime, and the writings of Newman (1972) and Coleman (1985 and 1988) provide examples of this. However, our knowledge of residential crime through official statistics is very incomplete. Official English statistics do record domestic burglary separately from other burglary and there is a category of theft in a dwelling, but other crimes which are frequently associated with residential areas are not separately identified as residential crime.

Despite our incomplete knowledge, a great deal of attention has been given to neighbourhood crime prevention, particularly to preventing burglary. The emphasis on residential burglary is partly due to the existence of official statistics which show that it is a major element in crime as a whole. It may also be that it is relatively easy to think of simple security devices to protect the home against break-ins.

Crime prevention advice has become almost ubiquitous through television and newspaper advertising and leaflets distributed by the police, insurance companies, building societies and banks. Few people will not have seen advice on fitting extra locks to doors and windows nor heard of neighbourhood watch schemes. An NOP survey reported that in 1987 31% of all homes in England and Wales had window locks compared with less than 10 per cent in 1980 (Crime Prevention News, 1987). A recent estimate for the number of neighbourhood watch schemes is 60 000 in only 6 years since the idea was first launched in Britain (Crime

Figure 1.1(a–c) These houses in Brooklyn, New York, display very high and obvious levels of physical security, and illustrate the extremes to which a fear-ridden society will go, perhaps with good reason.

(a)

(b)

(c)

Prevention News, 1989). Looking around residential areas in Britain in the last three or four years, it is surprising how many alarm boxes have been fitted to houses. On the medium- and high-rise flatted estates often associated with higher levels of crime there is plenty of evidence of increased security. Entrance lobbies to these blocks have been fitted with intercom controlled doors, and because these measures have often been abused and vandalized, there is an increasing use of closed-circuit television, security guards or receptionists to supervise access. Similarly many programmes of door strengthening and lock improvements have been carried out to individual flats.

We are perhaps fortunate that the demand for security has not gone as far as examples which can be found in the United States (see *Figure 1.1* of housing in Brooklyn, New York) but there are ample signs of a fortress society emerging in Europe. *Figure 1.2* illustrates the increasing use of grilles at windows, high-intensity outside lighting, alarms and even TV surveillance in London.

Despite this widespread increase in home security there seems little indication that these efforts have significantly reduced the problem of residential crime. It is true that some modestly successful reductions in crime have been achieved on some housing estates (see for example Poyner, Webb and Woodall, 1986; Poyner and Webb, 1987; Forrester, Chatterton and Pease, 1988). There was some evidence during the preparation of this book that the overall growth in officially reported crime had at least temporarily halted, with the figures for domestic burglaries showing a small drop. However, there is no sign of any sustained decline, and there is a long way to go before we can return to the crime levels of the late 1940s and early 1950s.

The thesis of this book is that the most reliable way to prevent crime in residential neighbourhoods is by design. The book presents evidence to show that once housing areas have certain design and layout characteristics, then the levels of crime can be very low indeed. The book focuses exclusively on low-rise housing. Although it is probably true that currently our most serious crime problems occur in poorer public sector housing estates, often involving medium- and high-rise housing forms, it seems likely that the kind of new housing which will predominate over the next ten or twenty years will be low-rise housing built by the private sector for sale and rent. It is in low-rise housing that it appears possible to design an environment in which informal social relationships can be reinforced to deter potential criminals and in which individuals and families can more easily police or guard their own property.

The material presented in the following chapters is based on research carried out by the authors while working at the Tavistock Institute of Human Relations. Following work for an earlier book called *Design against Crime* (Poyner, 1983), also published by Butterworths, research seemed to suggest that the design and layout of housing might be an important

Figure 1.2(a, b) There are signs that Europe is also moving towards a similar 'fortress society'. These photographs of two houses in the same Hampstead street show the use of a variety of security equipment such as window grilles, outdoor spotlights, alarms, and TV cameras.

(a)

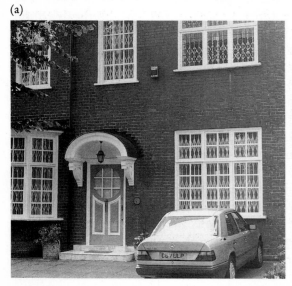

(b)

factor in the control of crime. A proposal was made and accepted by the Home Office to fund a study during 1983–85 to look at the layout of residential areas and its influence on crime.

The original study (Poyner, Helson and Webb, 1985) had two broad aims: to find out more about the nature of residential crime and to explore some aspects of housing layout that were believed to influence crime. To find out more about residential crime it was decided to look at the pattern of crime in a medium sized town which had a well-established town centre, some industrial and commercial areas and a wide variety of old and new suburbs. The town selected was Northampton. It was sufficiently well away from London to be more representative of typical British suburban housing including large areas of modern housing. A 10% sample of all crime reported in Northampton during 1982 was obtained from police files. A 10% sample was chosen on the assumption that this would yield at least 1000 crimes, which was considered appropriate for the manual classification of crime which the researchers had in mind. In the event the sample produced 1261 crimes within the urban area of Northampton.

Previous research had speculated about the increased vulnerability of houses on through roads, on exposed corners, end houses, those with access around the back of the house and those next to open land. It was hoped that such variations of layout could be examined methodically and so, in addition to Northampton, a large area of relatively uniform housing was chosen to analyse these variables. The area selected was part of Harrow in North London. Most of this housing was built in the 1920s and 1930s at the time when the London Underground was being improved and extended. It represents a very familiar form of English owner-occupied middle-income suburban housing (*Figure 1.3*), and because of its close proximity to London it was expected to have a comparatively high crime rate. Although these were the main reasons for selecting four wards of the Borough of Harrow, a further ward to the north called Stanmore Park was added, as this was an area of high-income group housing of the same period which it was thought might provide a different crime pattern. It had been shown by Maguire and Bennett (Maguire, 1982) that the pattern of burglary in such an area was different from that in middle- and lower-income housing. For these five wards of Harrow all crimes reported in 1982 were extracted and summarized from police files.

Figure 1.3 (a) Suburban housing in Harrow, North London built during the great house-building boom of the 1920s and 1930s. (b) A good example of a Harrow house still in its original condition.

(a)

(b)

By studying the police reports and by visiting the locations of crimes in the Harrow sample, it was easy to understand why individual houses might have been easy to break into because of some obvious weakness in access or surveillance, but it was difficult to identify siting or layout characteristics which would discriminate clearly between low- and high-risk houses. It seemed that most houses were equally vulnerable. However, in Northampton, where the housing was much more varied in its design and layout, the crime patterns which emerged showed significant differences in the distribution of crime between different areas of housing. Visits to the sites of specific crimes appeared to support this conclusion and showed that differently designed groups of housing had quite different crime problems. Unfortunately, because the data available for Northampton was limited to the 10% sample of a year's crime there was insufficient information to demonstrate these conclusions in a convincing way, particularly for burglary, which was poorly represented in the sample data.

In the two years which followed the completion of the first study in 1985, a good deal of effort was given by various bodies to the production of formal guidance to the building industry on crime prevention for housing, spurred on by Prime Ministerial pressure on all sectors of government and industry to work together on the prevention of crime. The British Standards sub-committee completed its work on Part 1 of its Guide on domestic security (British Standards Institution, 1986), a working group set up by the Standing Conference on Crime Prevention produced a report on security for inner city housing (Home Office, 1986a) and the National House-Building Council produced a set of guidelines for the house-building industry (NHBC, 1986). The main thrust of these guidance documents was that the security of doors and windows should be increased, but the NHBC guidance did break new ground by stressing the importance of a more secure site layout and introducing the issue of preventing autocrime as well as burglary.

Although these guidance documents summarized the current opinion on the best practice for crime prevention in housing, the authors of this book believed that the importance of layout had not been fully recognized. It seemed important to clarify and develop the findings of the first study and publish more developed guidance on crime and housing layout.

Efforts were made to fund further research so that more analysis could be made of crime patterns in the part of Northampton found to be promising in the first study. The authors would like to express their gratitude for financial support provided by Sir Clifford Chetwood, Chairman and Chief Executive of George Wimpey PLC, the Housing Research Foundation and to Mrs M.E. Pye and Mr Graham Pye for a grant from Mr and Mrs J.A. Pye's Charitable Settlement. This book is the result of their support and it describes the findings from both studies, setting out what the authors believe to be the most significant design features of low-rise housing which will enable future generations to live in a more crime free environment.

2 Residential crime

It is curious that in so much criminological literature we have never found any clear description of the crime associated with residential areas of a town or city. Maps of crime distribution are often plotted for specific geographical areas such as police divisions, local government areas and certainly at national level, but these all rely on police records and follow the police classifications of crime and administrative boundaries.

If we look at a typical distribution of crime in an urban area (see for example Baldwin and Bottoms, 1976: 58; and Brantingham and Brantingham, 1984: 232), the central areas show a much denser clustering of crime than in the surrounding areas. In part this higher density of crime at the centre represents the increased density of building and urban activity in the central area, but it also represents a different kind of criminal opportunity. The central area contains higher concentrations of shopping, drinking and entertainment facilities, and large parking lots including multi-storey parking, all of which are often associated with crime problems. The residential areas of a town or city occupy the much larger outer area. Although crime appears less dense in these areas it is clear that a good deal of urban crime is contained in residential areas. The problem is that it is unclear how far these are truly residential crimes and how far they might be associated with commercial, industrial or other activities.

The 1982 sample of crime drawn from the whole urban area of Northampton was classified into residential and non-residential crimes. Essentially, a crime was regarded as residential if it occurred in a mainly residential setting. Crimes which took place in pubs, shops or related car parks, even though they may have been in a residential area, were classified as non-residential. Crime relating to vehicles was regarded as residential if the vehicle was left in and around housing. In practice there were few definitional problems.

In previous crime prevention research we have often found that the categories used by the police and government statisticians are not a very satisfactory way of classifying criminal behaviour. They are too general and do little to define the nature of the behaviour involved. The UK Home Office statistics include categories such as 'theft from the person of another', 'theft from vehicles' and 'robbery', each

TABLE 2.1 A classification of crime in Northampton in 1982 into residential and non-residential crime

Crime category	Number	Percentage
Theft involving illegal entry (includes all burglary and some thefts in police records)		
Residential		
Burglary of dwellings	64	5.0
Failed attempted entries to dwellings	30	2.4
Gas/electric meters broken open	46	3.6
Theft and break-ins from garages and sheds	18	1.4
	158	12.4
Non-residential		
Shops burglary	27	2.1
Burglary of offices and other commercial premises	62	4.9
Schools burglary	22	1.7
Other burglaries	24	1.9
	135	10.6
Theft not involving illegal entry		
Residential		
Inside the home and other residential accommodation	30	2.4
In space around the house or communal areas (includes bicycles)	71	5.6
	101	8.0
Non-residential		
In pubs/discos/restaurants	11	0.9
Purses/wallets stolen in public places	13	1.0
Bicycles stolen in public places	40	3.2
Shoplifting	83	6.6
Theft from building sites	19	1.5
Various other thefts on business premises	63	5.0
Other thefts in public places	17	1.3
	246	19.5
Violent crime		
Domestic violence	6	0.5
Disputes in non-domestic context	36	2.8
Robbery/snatches in public places	6	0.5
Sexual attacks/incidents in public places	14	1.1
Other violence	7	0.6
	69	5.5
Criminal damage		
Residential		
Various	18	1.4
Non-residential		
Shop windows	15	1.2
Other damage	29	2.3
Fire setting	8	0.6
	70	5.6

TABLE 2.1 Continued

Crime category	Number	Percentage
Vehicle crime		
Residential		
Theft of cars	63	5.0
Theft of motorcycles	17	1.3
Theft of property or components from cars	68	5.4
Criminal damage to cars	16	1.3
Other residential vehicle crime	3	0.2
	167	13.2
Non-residential		
Theft of cars	64	5.1
Theft of motorcycles	13	1.0
Theft of property or components from cars	52	4.1
Damage to vehicles	17	1.3
Other theft from vehicles	45	3.6
	191	15.1
Other categories of crime		
Deception	50	4.0
Receiving/handling	16	1.3
Other	26	2.1
Insufficient information to classify	32	2.5
	124	9.9
Total number of crimes included in classification	1261	100.0

(Source: Poyner, Helson and Webb, 1985)

of which include a wide variety of different types of activity. The reasons for these categories are embedded in the historical development of the law rather than being designed to give a clear description of crime. Similar problems exist in other countries. For example, federal statistics in the USA are simplified into seven main categories to facilitate a collection of national statistics (uniform crime reports). Even common terms like burglary mean slightly different things in the different English-speaking countries and such comparisons become even more difficult with other languages and legal traditions. In an effort to by-pass some of the anomalies of official definitions and practices, the crime records have been reclassified in *Table 2.1* to give a more specific behavioural description of crime.

As indicated above, some of these categories differ considerably from the original police classification of crime. For example, theft from a gas or electricity meter is identified as a separate category since it has become recognized as a problem in its own right even though some cases will have been classified by the police as burglary and others will have been recorded as theft. Similarly, theft and break-ins to garages and sheds were classified by the police under several categories:

burglary, non-residential;
burglary of dwelling;
theft, non-residential;
theft of pedal cycle;
theft elsewhere;
other theft elsewhere.

It is clear from this that any conventional analysis of crime records would not have revealed this category. It would have been lost among these miscellaneous headings.

The information in *Table 2.1* is a simplified version of what appeared in the original study report, but even so it is still difficult to take in at first glance. *Table 2.2* attempts to simplify the information still further.

TABLE 2.2 Percentage distribution of crime in Northampton in 1982 into broad categories

Group of crimes	Residential (%)	Non-residential (%)
Theft involving illegal entry/burglary	12.5	10.7
Theft without illegal entry to buildings	8.0	19.5
Violent crime	0.5	5.0
Criminal damage	1.4	4.1
Vehicle crime	13.2	15.1
Other categories	–	9.9
	35.6	64.3

(Source: Poyner, Helson and Webb, 1985)

Generally, this distribution of crime in Northampton follows closely the national statistics for England and Wales in 1982. Residential burglary was about 12.5% of the national crime figure, the same as the equivalent figure in *Table 2.2*. The national figure for vehicle crime was 24.5% in 1982 and the figure from this sample in Northampton was only a little higher at 28%. Violent crime is about the same proportion as the national figure of 5.1% but criminal damage recorded in Northampton is much lower than the national figure of 12.8%. It is not surprising that criminal damage is the less reliable comparison because it is generally accepted that it is a very much under-recorded crime.

Since the figures in *Table 2.2* do approximate to the national distribution of crime we can assume that, nationally, residential crime makes up about a third of all reported crime. The main constituents of residential crime are theft involving illegal entry (burglary) and vehicle crime (autocrime) with a third category of theft not involving illegal entry also being important. There is comparatively little reported criminal damage in housing and there is little reported evidence of violent crime associated with housing. In fact the only violent incidents reported in residential settings are domestic disputes. Domestic violence is a problematic area for the police as it has long been uncertain how far the police should become involved in domestic disputes. It is almost certain that recent attention to this matter will lead to increased reporting to the police, much as there has been an increase in the reporting of rape.

Having identified the main elements of residential crime, it is important to recognize that these proportions do vary with the character of the areas and the form of housing. *Table 2.3* shows a comparison of residential crime in Northampton and Harrow. It is taken from data obtained during the first study. To facilitate a comparison between the two areas, the number of crimes are expressed as crimes per 1000 dwellings per year.

The table shows that the different housing environments can produce very different crime profiles. Harrow had more illegal entry to houses, amounting to nearly a third of residential crime. However, there were very few meter thefts compared with Northampton. Almost certainly this reflected socio-economic differences in that far fewer households in a mainly middle-income suburb of London would use coin-operated meters.

There was also a major difference in the amount of theft not involving illegal entry. There was more theft inside dwellings in Northampton because of theft in residential institutions which did not occur in the Harrow data. The differences in theft outside the house may also be due to different crime reporting practices. For example, the Northampton data includes theft of milk from doorsteps but such crimes are rarely recorded by the Metropolitan Police.

The figures for residential vehicle crime showed a much higher rate for Northampton, almost double the rate for Harrow. In many ways this might be surprising to those expecting a London suburb, with extensive on-street parking, to have serious problems of vehicle crime. Bearing in mind that the British Crime Survey has shown that the theft of cars

TABLE 2.3 Comparison of residential crime in Northampton and Harrow in 1982 (crimes/1000 dwellings/year)

Crime category	Northampton	Harrow
Theft involving illegal entry		
Burglary of dwellings	11.2	16.8
Failed attempted entries	5.3	4.7
Gas/electric meters broken open	8.1	0.4
Garages and sheds	3.2	2.6
	27.8	24.5
Theft not involving illegal entry		
Inside the home/residential accommodation	5.3	1.4
In space around house in communal areas	12.3	3.2
	17.6	4.6
Violent crime		
Domestic violence	1.1	0.4
Criminal damage		
Various	3.2	5.3
Vehicle crime		
Theft of cars	11.0	6.3
Theft of motorcycles	3.0	1.0
Theft from cars	11.9	6.5
Criminal damage to cars	2.8	3.2
Other vehicle crime	0.5	0.2
	29.3	17.2
All residential crime	78.8	52.0

(Source: Poyner, Helson and Webb, 1985)

is recorded quite accurately by the police (Hough and Mayhew, 1985), it seems reasonable to assume that the difference between the reported rates of vehicle crime in Northampton and Harrow reflects a real difference in crime levels.

The net effect of these differences in residential crime rates is that Northampton had an overall residential crime rate of about one-and-a-half times that for Harrow. The discovery that a town like Northampton had a more serious residential crime problem than an established London suburb was a surprise to the researchers, and it supports our belief that the control of crime in low-rise housing should be an important part of any national crime prevention policy.

3 The research studies

Before the research described in the book was begun, the only literature which dealt with housing design and crime was on burglary. The main focus of this burglary research was to describe the crime and the offenders. Research studies used several sources such as surveys of victims (Waller and Okihiro, 1978) and data from police files and from interviews with incarcerated burglars (Maguire, 1982). The most recent major UK work on burglary based most of its information on interviews with burglars (Bennett and Wright, 1984). The most important factor which was found to determine the risk of burglary was 'occupancy'. Burglary tended to take place when houses were temporarily empty and showed no signs of being occupied. However, what also began to emerge was the idea that some houses were more vulnerable to burglary because of their design or siting. Winchester and Jackson (1982) were able to show that the risk of burglary differed considerably between detached and terraced houses or semi-detached. They also found that factors such as being set back from the road, being adjacent to open space, having access from front to back of the house and not being overlooked all increased the risk of burglary. A summary of the design implications of this literature was given in *Design against Crime* (Poyner, 1983).

Because these ideas about the design and siting of houses had not been the main focus of previous research studies on burglary, we set out to develop this aspect further and look at the question of what characteristics of the design and layout of houses made them most vulnerable. It was hoped that the large area of mainly semi-detached housing in Harrow would provide a 'laboratory' in which to test the various design factors which might be contributing to vulnerability.

An important part of the method used in this research was to visit the locations of crimes and add important environmental data to the information already obtained from police files. As locations were visited it soon became clear to us that victimized houses had very obvious vulnerable features. For example, of 32 houses in Harrow from which higher value burglaries of luxury goods had been taken, 26 were large detached houses with ample space at the side to allow access to the back. Eight of the houses were corner

Figure 3.1 These large plots, some of which back on to open land, give plenty of easy access to the sides and rears of detached houses. (Source: Ordnance Survey (adapted).)

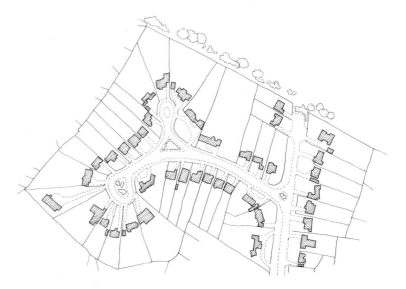

houses with the side of the plot exposed to the side road. Seven had gardens backing on to open ground. Most of these houses were located in Stanmore Park and *Figure 3.1* shows a section of map which included some of these victimized houses and shows how accessible are many of the plots.

A more precise sample of 70 semi-detached houses which had all been victims of burglaries in which electric goods such as televisions and video equipment had been taken was examined for vulnerability. Thirty-eight of these houses had been entered at the rear or side of the house and they were found to have the vulnerability characteristics shown in *Table 3.1*.

Armed with what we believed were useful indications of vulnerability, we set out to assemble some statistical evidence to show that victimized houses tended to be more vulnerable

TABLE 3.1 Vulnerability of burgled houses (electrical goods) in Harrow entered from the side or rear

Vulnerable feature	Number	Percentage
Shared driveway between houses	18	47
Space at the side of the house	5	13
One side of the rear garden exposed (corner houses, etc.)	10	26
No obvious vulnerability factor	5	13
	38	100

(Source: Poyner, Helson and Webb, 1985)

than non-victimized houses. Shared driveways seemed to be a particularly vulnerable design feature, giving access to the side and rear garden, as the house illustrated previously in *Figure 1.3(b)* shows. The map in *Figure 3.2* illustrates how extensive this particular design feature is in Harrow. By taking from Ordnance Survey maps of Harrow a random selection of map squares (100×100 m) we found that out of 1199 semi-detached houses in the sample, 577 (48%) had shared driveways. This was virtually the same proportion as in the sample of victimized houses above. The fact emerged that at least in respect of shared driveways the victimized sample of houses were no more vulnerable than the houses in the area as a whole, and we could not conclude from this that shared driveways increased the risk of burglary.

We tried a more refined analysis in which houses were classified as vulnerable or non-vulnerable. They were judged vulnerable if they had any form of weak access point, i.e. side access, corner houses, passageways at the side or back of the garden or shared driveway between houses. The result of this analysis was a little more encouraging in that the proportion of non-vulnerable houses in the random sample of houses was 30% compared with 13% in the victimized sample. This was the only analysis of vulnerability of houses that produced a statistically significant result (chi square $p<0.05$). Although this was evidence in support of our expectations, it was not good enough to develop clear guidance for the housing industry.

Crises such as this are not uncommon in research and usually lead to the development of a new approach to the problem in question. The approach we had adopted focused on the vulnerability of individual houses. It was an approach

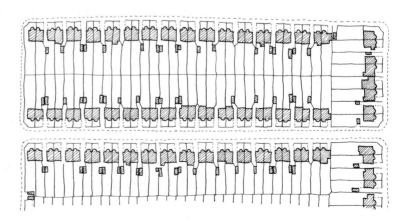

Figure 3.2 A large amount of housing in Harrow consists of semi-detached houses with shared driveways which leaves the sides of houses open, giving easier access to the rear garden. A house with a shared driveway is shown in *Figure 1.3(b)*. (Source: Ordnance Survey (adapted).)

adopted by other researchers too, because it lends itself to simple numerical analysis, and data for such an approach is readily to hand. What this analysis of individual house vulnerability was telling us was that all the houses in this area of Harrow were more or less equally vulnerable. Any differences in the layout or siting of individual houses were relatively unimportant in determining their selection by burglars as a target.

In addition to our visits to the locations of crime in Harrow, we had also completed many visits to crime locations in Northampton. One particularly familiar pattern began to emerge in the case of autocrime. Almost all the cases visited turned out to be thefts or damage which occurred in the communal parking areas in the housing built by the New Town Development Corporation. For the most part, housing in these developments was made up of narrow-fronted terraces with footpath access and parking in communal areas sometimes in front of houses but more often behind or at the end of terraces. It occurred to us that we had been focusing our analysis on the wrong level of design and that a more useful approach would be to look at the design characteristics of an area or group of houses rather than characteristics of individual houses.

The problem with our selection of Harrow as a site for research was that there was not enough differentiation between the various areas. This was due mainly to the fact that most of the area was developed over a comparatively short period in the great house-building boom of the 1930s. However, housing areas in Northampton had a very different history. There were many stages of development. Clustered around the town centre are street after street of late nineteenth-century terraces associated with the earlier industrial prosperity of Northampton due in part to its famous footwear industry. Beyond these terraces are patches of housing development corresponding to all phases of housing design from 1920 to the present day, except for the medium- and high-rise estates of the 1960s and early 1970s.

A section of north-east Northampton was chosen for closer study as it seemed to have somewhat more crime than other suburban areas and at the same time represented a particularly good cross-section of all these housing developments. The area was then carefully mapped to separate the different stages of development, each of which tended to have a different set of design relationships. This mapping of housing areas produced a very clear patchwork of different housing areas.

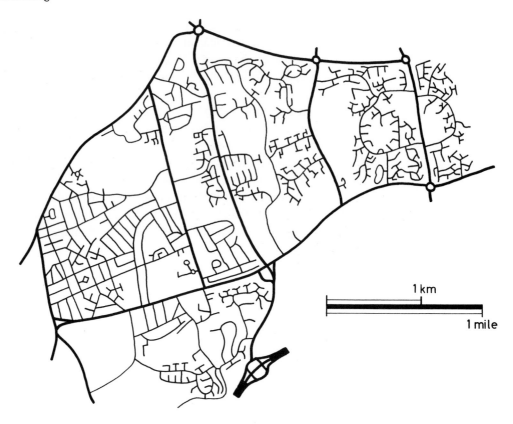

Figure 3.3 Street pattern of the north-east part of Northampton studied in this research. (Source: Abstract from street layout plan.)

When all crime was plotted onto these areas it was clear that some had much more crime than others. Clearest of all was the plot of autocrime which showed that the areas of housing which were vulnerable to this kind of crime were the New Town Corporation developments (as expected) and the terraced streets. No doubt the fact that cars in these areas were parked on the street or in separate communal parking areas had much to do with this distribution of crime.

The problem with this mapping of crime onto areas of housing development was that the sample of crime we had assembled for Northampton in the first study was too small to generate very reliable map distributions and so, although a number of conclusions were drawn from this data, it was clear that a much larger sample would be preferred. It was not until further funding was obtained that such an analysis could be carried out.

Once additional funds had been provided, the Chief Constable for Northamptonshire kindly agreed to give us access to the crime data, but with the introduction of computer-based crime data since the first study, it had become more difficult to obtain information because of the

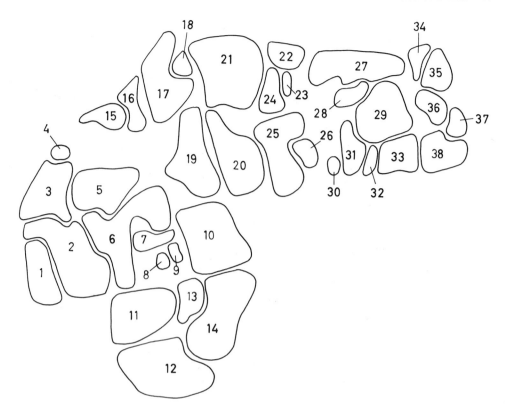

Figure 3.4 The 38 different areas of housing layout used in the analysis.

Data Protection Act. Unlike the earlier stage of the study we were restricted in access to specific addresses of victims. We had to compromise with approximate location information. This was good enough for locating crimes within the areas on our map but it did not allow us to identify individual houses at risk.

In the time between the first and second studies further development had taken place in Northampton, with more housing having been built in the north-eastern part of the town which we had studied in detail. Also the original study area crossed over between two police sub-divisions and so to up-date and simplify the research effort for the second stage the study area was restricted to the Weston Favell police sub-division, but extended to include newer housing not included in the first study. This revised area is shown in *Figure 3.3,* indicating the general street pattern.

Figure 3.4 shows the same area divided into 38 housing areas each with different forms of layout. In effect, these separate areas of housing layout were either built by different developers or, in the case of public sector housing, designed at different stages and probably by different teams.

The housing areas

The 38 separate housing areas shown in *Figure 3.4* vary in size from a small group of 32 houses in area 4 to areas 2 and 21 with 1013 and 1159 houses, respectively. The total number of houses in the 38 areas is 13 979 and the average number of houses in each area is 368. When we began work on this form of analysis we hoped that the areas of housing would classify into four or five basic types of housing layout; for example 1920s, post-war and new town public sector housing, and 1930s and modern private sector development. However, further research work with the new data revealed far more complex differences between the areas and although some are similar, most have important unique features which lead to differences in the distribution of crime.

To avoid tedium for both readers and authors we do not intend giving full descriptions of all 38 housing areas. All we can do here is to briefly illustrate some of the differences and leave the more detailed analysis to the discussion of different crimes in the following chapters. The five photographs in *Figures 3.5–3.9* illustrate the contrasting nature of five housing areas.

Area 2 – This council housing estate built in the 1920s is the second largest area. Housing is a mixture of semi-detached and short terraces facing similar houses across the street. These houses have small front gardens with low front fences but no side gates between terraces or pairs of houses. Rear gardens have little fencing in good repair. Cars are parked only on the street. A process of gentrification has recently begun in this area. Some of the houses are now owner-occupied and have had improvements made such as the fitting of replacement doors and windows, and stone cladding on the house facade.

Area 20 – Terraced housing built in the 1960s by the New Town Corporation all with footpath access to fronts and along the rear of back gardens. There are no front gardens, only shallow open fronts. Each house has a small enclosed garden at the rear with high walls or fences. Terraces are rarely arranged facing each other, but are more often planned as in *Figure 3.6* with fronts facing onto backs. Most parking is confined to communal parking courts unsupervised by housing.

Area 6 – This housing area was built during the 1930s. There are several long roads with mainly semi-detached houses, but there are also some terraces and bungalows. Access space at the side of the house is usually blocked by a garage or shed extension. Most houses have short driveways but cars are also parked on the street. Front gardens have low walls and houses face across the street.

Area 12 – This private sector housing was built during the 1960s. The houses are mostly semi-detached, with large windows facing each other across the street. The front gardens are open planned and all parking is on private driveways with garages. Access to rear gardens is normally through a full height gate at the side of the house. Open fronts are generally sparsely planted with small trees.

Area 38 – An area of housing not completed until after the first study. The houses are more individualistic and detached. They are planned at a variety of angles not always facing others. Houses have double garages often at right-angles to the house.

Figure 3.5 Typical view of area 2.

Figure 3.6 Typical view of area 20.

Figure 3.7 Typical view of area 6.

Figure 3.8 Typical view of area 12.

Figure 3.9 Typical view of area 38.

In effect, this north-eastern part of Northampton provides a wide range of the kind of housing found throughout the country and built over the last 70 years. It is this rich variety of housing that has made it possible to identify many of the effects design and layout can have on the risk and distribution of crime.

Crime data

The beat areas used by the police corresponded quite well to the boundaries of the housing areas in our analysis and so it was a comparatively easy matter to identify the crime records required for the second study. To economize on the research effort, only those crime codes likely to yield residential crime were requested. We also omitted the item of domestic disputes because it seemed unlikely to be related to design layout, and from the earlier research (*Table 2.1*) it was expected to be a very small item, amounting to less than 2% of reported residential crime.

TABLE 3.2 Crime data for north-east Northampton compared with data in *Table 2.3*

Crime category	Northampton 1987 No.	Northampton 1987	Northampton 1982	Harrow 1982
		Rates per 1000 households		
Theft involving illegal entry				
Burglary of in dwellings	416	29.8	11.2	16.8
Failed attempted entries	148	10.6	5.3	4.7
Gas/electric meters broken open	44	3.1	8.1	0.4
Garages and sheds	95	6.8	3.2	2.6
	703	50.3	27.7	24.5
Theft not involving illegal entry				
Inside the home/residential accommodation	102	7.3	5.3	1.4
In space around house or in communal areas	171	12.2	12.3	3.2
	273	19.5	17.5	4.6
Violent crime				
Domestic violence	*	*	1.1	0.4
Criminal damage				
Various	202	14.5	3.2	5.3
Vehicle crime				
Theft of cars	295	21.1	11.0	6.3
Theft of motor cycles	127	9.1	3.0	1.0
Theft from cars	515	36.9	11.9	6.5
Criminal damage to cars	75	5.4	2.8	3.2
Other vehicle crime	64	4.6	0.5	0.2
	1076	77.1	29.3	17.2
Totals	2254	161.4	78.8	52.1

* This information was not obtained from the police for 1987.

The crime records from the police computer were classified along similar lines to the earlier study, and we were surprised to discover that the residential crime rate for this area in 1987 amounted to more than double the rate for Northampton in 1982. This increase partly reflects the continued increase in reported crime, which had been rising by about 6% per annum nationally. It also indicates that this area of low-rise suburban housing has been deteriorating, in terms of crime, faster than the country as a whole.

Certainly no one could claim that this is a low-crime area or that it does not have serious crime problems. The new data for 1987 is summarized in *Table 3.2*, alongside data from the first study presented earlier in *Table 2.3*.

As can be seen from *Table 3.2*, there is a large sample of 2254 residential crimes available for use in this analysis and all the major crime problems known to us from the first study remain important. The greatest increase in crime is in theft from cars, but the rates for illegal entry (burglary) and the theft of cars have also increased. Overall the new data gives us a very good basis for further investigation of the distribution of crime across this part of Northampton.

4 Social and environmental factors

The predominant view about crime is that it is caused primarily by social factors. For example, poor education, unemployment, certain kinds of family upbringing, weak community structures, lack of rewarding recreational and community activity, are often thought to be responsible for producing criminals. In understanding the role of environmental design in crime it is difficult to ignore the claims that are made for social factors, and it is important to consider the relationship between the two.

A principal method of studying crime in this book is to map its distributions across areas with different layout designs. Many of these maps will show that more crime occurs in public sector housing estates than in owner-occupied housing. It would be claimed by many criminologists that this is because of the poorer social conditions in public sector housing. These estates experience more crime because more potential offenders live there.

There is a difficulty, however, in knowing how far the problem of crime on public sector estates is due to the kinds of people who live there or to the opportunities for crime provided by their environment. Researchers with different orientations have different points of view. There seems little doubt that Professor Alice Coleman believes that design is the cause of crime, and other anti-social behaviour (see Coleman, 1985). Extensive opposition to her views in, for example, the architectural press suggests that architects or their academic peers do not agree. They appear to take the view that such problems are not caused by architectural design but by more fundamental social and political policies (for example Lipman and Harris, 1988; and Ravetz, 1988). A similar view comes from the criminological establishment in the form of Professor Tony Bottoms who advocates the importance of housing allocation and allied policies in dealing with the problems of difficult public sector estates (Bottoms and Wiles, 1988).

It is very understandable why it is difficult to sort out whether it is environmental design or social policy which influences the occurrence of crime. The problem is that social factors and design tend to vary together. Just as there are

Figure 4.1 The distribution of theft of motorcycles in north-east Northampton, 1987.

socio-economic differences between owner-occupied housing and public sector housing estates, so there are differences in the way the two housing sectors have been designed and built. For example, the way owner-occupied housing provides for the motorcar is usually quite different from public sector housing. Private developers normally provide each house with its own car access with a driveway and a garage or garage space. In the public sector it is normal to separate car access from houses and provide communal parking bays, and if garages are provided they are more likely to be in separate blocks or in garage courts. In the private sector, houses without driveways would be more difficult to sell. The public sector does not have the constraint of a market and, with severe cost limits, it is not surprising that designers adopt different solutions. The differences in social structure and environmental design co-vary and it is logically difficult to separate the effect of design from social structure.

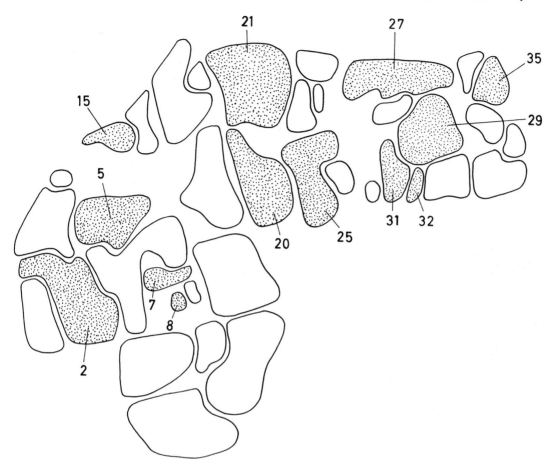

Figure 4.2 Housing areas in north-east Northampton which are predominantly public sector.

We would argue that design or opportunity factors are at least as important as social factors in influencing the occurrence of crime. One way to begin this discussion is to look at a map of the area which shows the distribution of theft of motorcycles throughout the 38 housing areas (*Figure 4.1*). Even though the map does not indicate the density of housing in each area, it appears to show that crime varies a good deal between the areas. Several of the housing areas, including some of the larger areas, have none of these crimes, while others have comparatively many. *Figure 4.2* shows which areas are composed of mainly public sector housing. It is clear from a comparison of the two maps that most of the motorcycles were taken from areas of public sector housing. Only a handful of thefts came from private sector housing.

What does this mean? If we believe in the social factors explanation, then presumably we would claim that the main reason for this distribution was that most potential offenders live on these estates and therefore the motorcycles that they steal are those readily to hand. Even when the thefts occur outside these estates they tend to be close by.

However the opportunity explanation is just as plausible. It seems likely that most motorcycles are owned by men in the lower income groups. If this is true, then it is reasonable to assume that most motorcycles in this part of Northampton will be kept on the public sector estates. It could be argued that it is the distribution of motorcycles that gives the crime distribution. It can, therefore, be argued both ways, that either the social or the opportunity factors are the main determinants of the pattern of theft. Indeed it could be argued that it is some mixture of the two explanations. However, when we look at some other types of crime the varying patterns of distribution help considerably to clarify the matter.

Table 4.1 compares the distribution of different types of crime among the housing areas of the study area. For each of five types of crime (motorcycle theft, meter break-ins, stolen cars, burglary and thefts from garages) the housing areas are arranged in rank order from the highest rate of crime to the lowest. Crime rates are calculated for all areas with 100 or more houses by simply dividing the number of crimes by the number of houses and multiplying by 1000 to give a crime rate per 1000 houses. In *Table 4.1* the housing areas which are public sector estates are marked with a blob (●).

The first column in *Table 4.1* shows what we already know from the maps in *Figures 4.1* and *4.2*, that the highest rate of motorcycle theft occurs in public sector housing. As the risk of theft is reduced the housing is less likely to be in the public sector. The ten areas with no motorcycle thefts are all at the bottom of the list and none are in the public sector.

Looking at all five columns in *Table 4.1*, it is clear that the distribution of public sector housing differs considerably between crime types. The first three columns all show that public sector areas are associated with the highest crime rates, but for burglary and garage theft the pattern is different. These columns show that the highest crime rates occur in owner-occupied housing. If we assume that most potential offenders for all kinds of crime live in the poorer public sector housing, then it is clear that they must regard opportunities for burglary and theft from garages as more attractive in other areas than in their own. If this is true it seems more likely that the pattern of crime distribution is determined by opportunities for crime than by the distribution of potential offenders.

If it is opportunity that is the more influential factor, then the reason why most cars are stolen from public sector areas must be due to increased opportunity for car theft in these areas than to the prevalence of offenders' homes. Certainly casual inspection of the study area reveals that there are many cars parked around public sector housing areas on the street and in communal parking bays with little or no supervision. By comparison, in most owner-occupied estates cars are less in evidence, being parked off the street on driveways or, no doubt, locked up in garages.

TABLE 4.1 Distribution of five different types of crime in 31 housing areas

Motorcycles			Meters			Cars stolen			Burglary			Garages		
cr	ha	psh	cr	ha	psh	cr	ha	psh	cr	ha	psh	cr	ha	psh
23	25	●	13	35	●	66	35	●	70	24		22	17	
22	29	●	10	25	●	50	29	●	47	11		16	14	
21	7	●	7	2	●	43	32	●	40	33		12	22	
20	35	●	6	27	●	41	21	●	33	28		8	1	
19	20	●	6	32	●	31	25	●	31	1		8	3	
19	26		5	5	●	27	7	●	31	10		6	16	
18	32	●	5	7	●	27	27	●	31	17		5	10	
15	21	●	4	21	●	24	20	●	30	20	●	5	19	
13	27	●	3	15	●	23	13		30	25	●	5	25	●
13	1		3	20	●	19	17		30	32	●	4	6	
8	19		3	29	●	19	19		30	35	●	4	27	●
7	33		0	1		16	5	●	29	22		3	11	
6	31	●	0	3		14	38		28	36		2	12	
6	2	●	0	6		13	1		26	19		2	20	●
5	5	●	0	10		12	15	●	26	29	●	2	33	
4	6		0	11		12	16		25	27	●	1	5	●
4	36		0	12		12	36		24	14		1	21	●
3	11		0	13		11	2	●	24	38		1	29	●
3	3		0	14		11	34		21	2	●	0	2	●
3	15	●	0	16		10	3		19	21	●	0	7	●
2	17		0	17		10	26		19	26		0	13	
0	10		0	19		7	24		16	13		0	15	●
0	12		0	22		6	11		12	3		0	24	
0	13		0	24		5	6		11	34		0	26	
0	14		0	26		5	12		10	5	●	0	28	
0	16		0	28		5	10		10	6		0	31	●
0	22		0	31	●	5	28		9	15	●	0	32	●
0	24		0	33		4	14		9	31	●	0	34	
0	28		0	34		4	22		7	12		0	35	●
0	34		0	36		2	33		0	16		0	36	
0	38		0	38		0	31	●	0	7	●	0	38	

Key
cr = crime rate (per 1000 households)
ha = housing area
psh = public sector housing (marked by ●)

Even the data on meter thefts can be seen to support our view that 'opportunity' provides a more satisfactory explanation for the distribution of crime than the location of offenders' homes. The crime rates for meter thefts show that they take place exclusively in public sector housing. No doubt many would see this as good evidence of socio-economic factors being of primary importance, suggesting that only people living in poor public sector housing conditions would be motivated to break into meters. They would only do this in their own neighbourhood because they would need local knowledge to know where the meters were. However, the opportunity explanation would be that meters were only installed in lower income households who find it difficult to manage the payment of bills. Therefore the opportunity for such crime only exists in this sector.

It is important to note that both opportunity and social explanations for crime assume that there will always be some members of an urban community who are sufficiently motivated to commit crime. The social explanation merely provides an explanation for this motivation or predisposition, and assumes that such motivated people will inevitably find an outlet for offending. The opportunity explanation insists that the availability of criminal opportunity is also necessary to offending. Motivation is not enough.

In residential areas, the relative importance of social factors and design can be summarized as follows. For crime to occur there must be a reasonable supply of potential offenders (and this is most likely to be provided by the presence of large areas of lower income housing), but in residential areas this will not lead to any significant amount of crime unless there is some form of opportunity provided by the environment. The role of the environment in determining the distribution of crime is to provide these opportunities. The thesis behind this book is that by methodically removing opportunities for crime, no matter how many potential offenders there are, crime will not occur. We hope to show that the opportunities that lead to residential crime are predominantly provided by the design and layout of housing. Careful design and layout can reduce the opportunities for crime and can therefore achieve crime free environments.

5 Car crime

Autocrime, unlike burglary, has largely escaped the research insights of criminologists. There has been little research on the nature of crime associated with vehicles and the motives or characteristics of the offenders. Even so the national statistics have reported the total number of thefts of or from vehicles to be about the same as the total number of burglaries, and recently a little greater (Home Office, 1988). The 1982 data on Northampton (*Table 2.1*) shows that vehicle crime amounted to 28% of the sample, a somewhat

TABLE 5.1 Detailed classification of residential vehicle crime in north-east Northampton, 1987

Crime type	Number of crimes	Rate per 1000 households
Theft of motor vehicles		
Cars	295	21.1
Motorcycles	127	9.1
Commercial vehicles	2	0.1
	424	30.3
Theft from motor vehicles		
Property left in cars	355	25.4
External car components	118	8.4
Petrol siphoned from car	36	2.6
Car batteries removed	6	0.4
Component removed from motorcycles	8	0.6
Property stolen from other vehicles	15	1.1
	538	38.5
Criminal damage to motor vehicles		
Car windows smashed	24	1.7
Car bodywork damaged	23	1.6
Car tyres slashed	9	0.6
Other car damage	19	1.4
Damage to other vehicles	14	1.0
Damage but type of vehicle not recorded	25	1.8
	114	8.1
Total residential vehicle crime	1076	76.9

higher percentage than burglary offences. Just under half of the vehicle crime occurred in residential situations.

Vehicle crime includes theft and damage of vehicles, and theft includes taking things from vehicles as well as taking the vehicle itself. A more descriptive classification of residential vehicle crime was developed which is shown in *Table 5.1*. The number of crimes in this table are those from the 1987 data for north-east Northampton, shown both as totals and as rates of crime per 1000 households.

From *Table 5.1* it is clear that the two main groups of vehicle crime are the theft of cars and the theft of property taken from inside cars, with the theft of motorcycles and of components removed from cars being the only other two groups of significant size.

The theft of cars

The crime of stealing cars distinguishes itself from most other types of theft in that most of the cars reported as stolen are recovered by the police. They are usually undamaged, but sometimes property or equipment such as a radio may be removed. Less often cars are found damaged in traffic accidents or even burnt out. In the case of cars stolen in our 1982 data, the percentage recovered in Harrow was 80% and in Northampton the figure was 89%. Autotheft is the only really good example of property marking that works. The registration of vehicles with their number plates seems to be the main reason why the police find lost cars. Occasionally they catch the thieves in possession.

Stealing cars, judging from our 1982 sample of crime in Northampton, is an exclusively male occupation. One of the difficulties of researching this type of offence is that few offenders are ever caught. Out of 127 car thefts the offenders were identified in only 22 or 17% – the national figure is 25%. A larger proportion of offenders were caught following residential car thefts than non-residential thefts which suggests that they tend to live in the same area. Their average age was 19 years, ranging from 14 to 29. In the sample, none was described as employed. Many were described, perhaps euphemistically, as 'scholars'. Most lived in Northampton but three were from Luton, two from the West Midlands and three had escaped from Nottingham prison.

Police records are very unclear about how cars might have been stolen, but it is frequently assumed that duplicate keys were used, presumably because cars were found undamaged. In one case a youth was disturbed making an attempt on a car and ran off, leaving a bunch of keys in the car unrecognized by the owners of the car. Where it can be deduced from the file, residential autotheft tends to take place during the evening, whereas thefts in non-residential areas occur as much during the day as at night. This may be because cars tend to be in non-residential settings such as car parks associated with shopping centres during the day and left in residential areas at night. The cars are usually found by police some time later, usually in the Northampton area, but sometimes some distance away.

There does not seem to be much evidence that cars are taken for their intrinsic value. Most are several years old and of comparatively low market value. Judging by the average age of those caught and the location and manner of discovery, most thefts seem to be made for the purpose of using a car for a limited period and then dumping it – perhaps when it runs out of petrol or because of some minor traffic accident. One or two cars seem to be stolen for use in other crime, and in this connection it should be pointed out that three or four cars were found burnt out, perhaps to destroy evidence such as fingerprints. One crime in the first sample was solved by the use of fingerprints found in a stolen car.

Car security

The conventional approach that has been adopted for the control of car theft has been the use of various security devices. Early cars had virtually no security. As the car evolved and became an everyday object, so security measures became normal practice. Cars were fitted with doors and doors were fitted with locks. The starting device was fitted with an ignition key instead of a push button. In more recent history as a measure against the continuing increase in theft, government legislation in a number of countries has insisted on the introduction of steering column locks (Federal Republic of Germany in the early 1960s and in the UK in 1971). More recently further efforts have been made to control these thefts by improving the specification of door locks and etching the car glazing with its registration number, and some further ideas have been put forward suggesting the use of electronics as well as developments in locking hardware (Southall and Ekblom, 1985).

Can further increases in car security significantly reduce crime? There are many reasons why security measures are unlikely to have much impact on the problem. First, there will always be users who do not use the security devices.

However many times they are exhorted to lock up their cars, there is always a minority who do not, whether they forget or become careless, or whatever the reason. Studies of locking behaviour in England a few years ago showed that between 10% and 20% of cars are left unlocked, and that older cars are more often left insecure than new cars (Riley and Mayhew, 1980). A second problem is that in time security devices become less effective due to wear or damage. Locks become loose, window closing devices work loose. It is also clear that the age group who seem interested in stealing cars soon finds methods to defeat the new technologies as they are introduced. After all, cars are ubiquitous objects in our society and young men have all kinds of legitimate opportunities to explore and experiment with them.

To look at the problem from a more statistical point of view, it is interesting to examine the effect of introducing steering column locks. This security device seemed to be a very good idea. It combined the ignition key with a lock to immobilize the steering wheel. There was every reason to believe that it would work because every car had to have one and the lock would work automatically as soon as the driver removed the ignition key from the car. No extra effort was required of an owner or driver and so compliance would not provide a problem. When these locks were introduced by law in Germany there was a marked drop in the theft of cars between 1960 and 1963 (from about 120 000 to under 50 000 per year). In the UK similar legislation was introduced in 1971 and it was hoped that a similar drop in car theft would follow. The innovation was carefully monitored by the Home Office and a paper was published in 1976 suggesting that, although there had been no immediate drop in crime following the introduction of steering column locks, as older cars without these locks were phased out and replaced by new cars it might be expected that the number of thefts would begin to fall (Mayhew *et al.*, 1976).

The national statistics on vehicle theft have not borne out this promised improvement. Vehicle theft has continued to increase almost every year to be more than three times as many 15 years later (Home Office, 1981 and 1988). What is more, the rate of theft has far outstripped the increase in population in the offender age group and the increase in car registrations, which is barely 50% more than it was 15 years ago. It should also be noted that these statistics are likely to be reliable because theft of cars, more than most other crimes, is regarded as accurately recorded by the police.

Bearing in mind that the steering column lock was seen at the time as being a very significant improvement in car security, which was likely to be very effective because it did not require a change of behaviour by users, we should be warned that future improvements may also show similarly disappointing results. The conclusion is not that security measures on cars are useless and should therefore be abandoned, but that it is doubtful that a dramatic reduction in car theft will result by merely increasing security.

Environmental protection

We would like to suggest that there is an alternative strategy to increasing security, which may in the long term provide a much more effective solution to residential car theft. If we now look at a geographical distribution of residential car theft we find that this type of crime does not exist equally in all kinds of housing layout. The map of housing areas in north-east Northampton is shown in *Figure 5.1*. The total of 295 residential car thefts which were reported in 1987 gives a

Figure 5.1 The distribution of theft of cars in north-east Northampton, 1987.

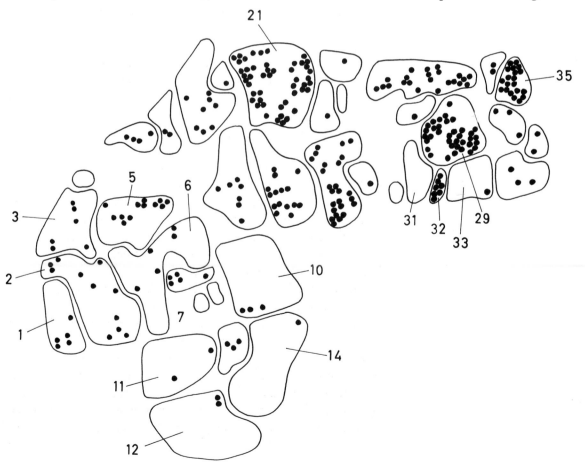

very clear visual pattern. There can be little doubt that although the housing areas vary in density to some extent, the distribution of car theft is highly selective. Several housing areas can be found with very little car theft, for example areas 10, 11, 12, 14. There are also heavily dotted areas such as 21, 25, 29 and 35.

As with the map of motorcycle thefts discussed in the last chapter (*Figure 4.1*), there is a tendency for the more heavily dotted areas to be public sector housing, even though car ownership would be if anything greater in the owner-occupied housing. However, an explanation based on tenure or similar social factors does not satisfactorily explain this map. For example, at the western end of the map areas 1, 2, 3, 5, 6 and 7 all seem to have similar densities of this crime even though 2, 5 and 7 are council estates, and 1, 3 and 6 are inter-war private sector estates.

More difficult to explain is the distribution of this crime in the cluster of areas 29, 31, 32 and 33. Of these 29 and 32 are covered with crime dots, whereas 31 and 33 are virtually free of car theft. As might be expected 29 and 32 are public sector housing estates. What is surprising is that 31 is also a public sector estate, but it had no theft of cars and gives the impresion that, like 33, it must be a private sector estate. There must be very compelling reasons why people steal cars from 29 and 32 but not from 31 and 33 which are right next to these crime-ridden areas. The reasons cannot include housing tenure or any other social factor.

In the first study which included data from Harrow it was thought that one possible explanation of the high levels of car theft in some areas and not in others was the availability of garages and so an analysis was made of the types of places cars

Figure 5.2 View of a typical communal parking area in new town public sector housing.

TABLE 5.2 Locations of car theft in Harrow and Northampton, 1982

Location	Harrow	Northampton
Garages*	1	2
Driveway/front hardstanding	5	2
Back alleyways	1	–
Parking areas/bays	2	9
Street outside house	54	31
Location not known	39	19
	102	63

*All three garages used to park cars were left open at the time, probably with the cars left unlocked as well.

(Source: Poyner, Helson and Webb, 1985)

were taken. The results of this analysis are set out in *Table 5.2.*

These findings seem to suggest that cars were reasonably safe in garages and for that matter on driveways, back alleyways and parking areas, but when parked on the street there was a much greater risk of theft. The problem with this analysis is that we could not be sure how the risk varied, because we did not know what proportion of parking was in garages, on driveways or in the street. To find out would have required a major survey of parked cars throughout Harrow and Northampton, which would have been a massive undertaking.

However the advantage of the analysis by housing areas is that we know the number of houses in each and can calculate some measure of density of crime per number of households and compare the effect of different types of layout design. When we look again at the areas with a heavy marking of dots, it soon becomes apparent that these are new town public sector housing areas with parking for cars kept separate in communal areas, often at the back of or further removed from the houses they serve (*Figure 5.2*). Other public-sector housing has less car theft and generally a more conventional layout with houses facing the street in which cars are parked (see *Figure 3.5*). The areas with little or no car theft all have some form of driveway or hardstanding in front of the houses, which in turn face the street (*Figure 5.3*).

To tabulate these differences more methodically, *Table 5.3* lists the housing areas with 100 or more houses in order of their risk of car theft from zero to a maximum of 66 thefts per

Figure 5.3 Private sector housing with cars parked on driveways or in garages.

1000 houses. The table also shows how a number of associated factors relate to this rank-ordered list.

The pattern of blobs shows how the presence or absence of the factors listed across the top of the table varies according to the area's rank in the table. To aid the visual presentation, the table is separated horizontally at the top of the table into three panels showing low-risk, medium-risk and high-risk areas. It is readily apparent from the table that in each of these groups there is a different pattern of factors. The low-risk areas at the top of the table are nearly all owner-occupied and all have driveways with houses facing the street. Most have garages but not quite all. By contrast the high-risk areas are nearly all public sector without driveways but with communal parking areas. Generally houses in the high-risk areas do not face the street. The medium-risk areas tend to be more like the low-risk areas but there are fewer houses with driveways or garages and more parking on the street.

Although tenure would show up in a statistical analysis as strongly correlated to theft, the anomalies mentioned previously show up in this table. The lowest risk area (area 31) is in the public sector and so are three of the medium-risk areas. Unlike the findings from the first study in *Table 5.2*, street parking does not seem to be a strongly influential variable compared with the presence of driveways or communal parking areas. Garages are generally associated with low-risk areas but they do not seem as necessary as driveways. Indeed, area 31 had no garage provision, only hardstandings in front of houses. A feature which also seemed to be related to risk of theft was the extent to which houses faced onto the street. Where they did, the risk was lowest. Where they did not face the street, the risk was highest.

The best explanation for the distribution of crime in *Figure 5.1* seems to be that design has a major influence over the occurrence of theft. If there are driveways to each house and the houses face the street there are unlikely to be many car thefts. *Figure 5.4* illustrates diagrammatically the kind of layout which has high and low car theft.

TABLE 5.3 An analysis of the environmental factors influencing theft of cars

Area	Crime rates	Owner-occupied	Driveways	Garage	Street parking	Communal parking	Facing street	Through footways
31	0	–	●●●	–	●	–	●●●	●●●
33	2	●●●	●●●	●	–	–	●●●	●●●
22	4	●●●	●●●	●●●	–	–	●●●	–
14	4	●●●	●●●	●●●	–	–	●●●	●●●
12	5	●●●	●●●	●●●	–	–	●●●	–
10	5	●●●	●●●	●●●	–	–	●●●	●●●
6	5	●●●	●●●	●●	●●●	–	●●●	●
28	5	●●●	●●	●●	–	–	●●	●●
11	6	●●●	●●	●●	●●	–	●●●	●●●
24	7	●●●	●●●	●●●	–	–	●●	●●●
3	10	●●●	●	●	●●●	–	●●●	●●
26	10	●●●	●●●	●●●	–	–	●●●	●●●
1	10	●●●	–	●	●●●	–	●●●	●●
34	11	●●●	●●●	●●	●	–	●●●	–
2	11	–	–	–	●●●	–	●●●	●●
16	12	●●●	●●●	●●●	–	–	●●●	–
15	12	–	–	●●	●●	–	●●●	–
36	12	●●●	●●●	●●●	–	–	●	●●●
38	14	●●●	●●●	●●●	–	–	●●●	–
5	16	–	–	●	●●●	–	●●●	–
17	19	●●●	●●	●●	●	–	●●●	●
19	19	●●●	●●	●●●	●	–	●●●	●●
13	23	●●	●	●	●●	–	●●●	–
20	24	–	–	–	●	●●●	–	●●●
7	27	–	●●	●	●●	–	●●●	●
27	27	–	–	●	–	●●●	–	●●●
25	31	–	●	●	–	●●●	●	●●●
21	41	–	–	●	–	●●●	–	●●●
29	50	–	–	–	–	●●●	–	●●●
32	43	–	–	–	–	●●●	–	●●●
35	66	–	–	–	–	●●●	–	●●●

●●● indicates that the factor is fully present and ●● and ● indicate some intermediate value. The dash (–) indicates that the factor is not present.

The rate for this table is the number of thefts per 1000 households in each of the housing areas with over 100 houses.

Figure 5.4 These diagrams illustrate the characteristics of housing areas with high and low risk of car theft.

promotes car theft   prevents car theft

Property taken from inside cars

Removing property from inside cars is an easier crime to commit than moving the car since it only requires opening an insecure car or breaking into a locked one. The point made above about cars being left insecure may well account for many of these thefts, but victims only rarely admit to leaving their cars unlocked. Most often the police find no sign of forced entry and assume that a duplicate key was used or record no details about entry. In a few cases forced entry is made which occasionally involves the smashing of a window. It is perhaps this apparent ease of access that has led to theft from vehicles increasing at a much faster rate than car theft. While the theft of vehicles has only increased modestly in the last ten years, thefts from vehicles has more than doubled (Home Office, 1988). This point is reinforced by the data in *Table 3.2* for north-east Northampton in 1987 which shows that theft from cars has emerged as by far the largest group of residential crimes.

Despite this abundance of reported incidents, we know very little about the offenders because relatively few are caught. Nationally only 21% of these crimes are solved (Home Office, 1988). In our 1982 Northampton sample of crime, of 48 incidents of theft from cars in residential settings the police had discovered the culprits in only two cases. They were young men aged 17 and 18, respectively, both with previous convictions.

The items removed can vary from clothing and money to small components such as indicator switches, but the most popular items were tools, tool boxes, tax discs, radio and stereo equipment. Sometimes, thieves seem to have been rather desperate to find anything worthwhile taking from the car with items reported stolen such as sunglasses, an ice scraper and even a bag of cat litter (our research assistant suggested it might have been a cat burglar!). Although many of these crimes seem rather trivial, they are clearly a nuisance to the car owners, otherwise they would not have bothered to report them to the police.

There is clearly scope for better security of cars, and owners should perhaps take more care to lock up and avoid leaving items in the cars, but it seems clear that even with a much more security conscious public there is unlikely to be dramatic reductions in this kind of crime. Over the last year or two there have been many campaigns to publicize security of cars and yet this crime is still increasing very quickly. Could it be that the design of our residential environments could provide more effective protection?

If we look at the map distribution of theft from inside cars, which is presented in *Figure 5.5*, it is possible to see that although there are more incidents the general pattern is similar to the distribution of car theft in *Figure 5.1*. However, a closer comparison between the maps shows that some areas with virtually no car theft have quite a lot of theft of property from cars, for example areas 31 and 33.

We can use the same tabulation technique as in *Table 5.3* and arrange the housing areas in rank order of theft from cars. *Table 5.4* shows the results of this analysis.

The pattern is very similar to that of *Table 5.3* in respect of driveways, garages, street parking, communal parking areas and houses facing the street. The crime occurs most often in layouts with parking away from the houses. However the presence of driveways does not seem to be quite such a strong factor in this type of crime. Interestingly this ties up with data we obtained from the first study. As can be seen from *Table 5.5*, the locations of thefts from inside cars in that study showed that some thefts took place on driveways.

This information does help to explain why the theft from cars is somewhat more widespread on the map in *Figure 5.5*. It would seem that cars are a little more vulnerable to theft of property from inside when close to houses or on driveways and hardstandings than they are to being stolen. This is easily imagined when we consider that the task of stealing from a car is easier than driving it away. Starting up a car would attract far more attention in a residential setting than just trying a car door or tampering with the lock.

After a careful search through the data on the various housing areas and an analysis of the planning features of those areas where thefts were comparatively uncommon, one factor emerged which seemed to explain the difference between the

TABLE 5.4 An analysis of the environmental factors influencing theft from inside cars

Area	Crime rates	Owner occupied	Driveways	Garage	Street parking	Communal parking	Facing street	Through footways
16	0	•••	•••	•••	–	–	•••	–
22	4	•••	•••	•••	–	–	•••	–
7	5	–	••	•	••	–	•••	•
34	5	•••	•••	••	•	–	•••	–
38	5	•••	•••	•••	–	–	•••	–
17	7	•••	••	••	•	–	•••	•
13	8	••	•	•	••	–	•••	–
15	9	–	–	••	••	•	•••	–
5	10	–	–	•	•••	•	•••	–
12	10	•••	•••	•••	–	–	•••	–
3	13	•••	•	•	•••	–	•••	••
10	13	•••	•••	•••	–	–	•••	•••
33	15	•••	•••	•	–	–	•••	•••
6	16	•••	•••	••	•••	–	•••	•
19	16	•••	••	•••	•	–	•••	••
36	16	•••	•••	•••	–	–	•	•••
28	22	•••	••	••	–	•	••	••
11	24	•••	••	••	••	–	•••	•••
25	24	–	•	•	–	•••	•	•••
2	25	–	–	–	•••	–	•••	••
24	27	•••	•••	•••	–	–	••	•••
14	28	•••	•••	•••	–	–	•••	•••
26	29	•••	•••	•••	–	–	•••	•••
27	29	–	–	•	–	•••	–	•••
20	31	–	–	–	•	•••	–	•••
29	33	–	–	–	–	•••	–	•••
1	34	•••	–	•	•••	–	•••	••
31	35	–	•••	–	•	–	•••	•••
21	37	–	–	•	–	•••	–	•••
32	43	–	–	–	–	•••	–	•••
35	73	–	–	–	–	•••	–	•••

••• indicates the general presence of a factor and •• and • indicate the partial presence of a factor. A dash (–) indicates that the factor is not present.
The rate for this table is the number of thefts per 1000 households in each of the housing areas with over 100 houses.

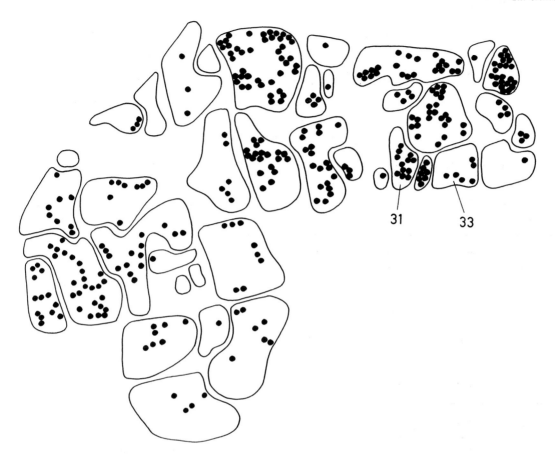

31 33

Figure 5.5 The distribution of theft from inside cars in north-east Northampton, 1987.

two distributions quite well. Both *Tables 5.3* and *5.4* show a seventh column labelled 'through footways'. For theft from the car there is a very good correlation with this variable but the pattern does not occur for the theft of cars. There are a number of pathway systems running through the study area

TABLE 5.5 Locations of theft from inside cars in Northampton and Harrow, 1982

Location	Northampton	Harrow
Garage	1	3
Driveways/hardstanding at front	4	13
Back alleyways	1	2
Communal parking areas/bays	17	1
Street	15	42
Location not known	10	23
	48	84

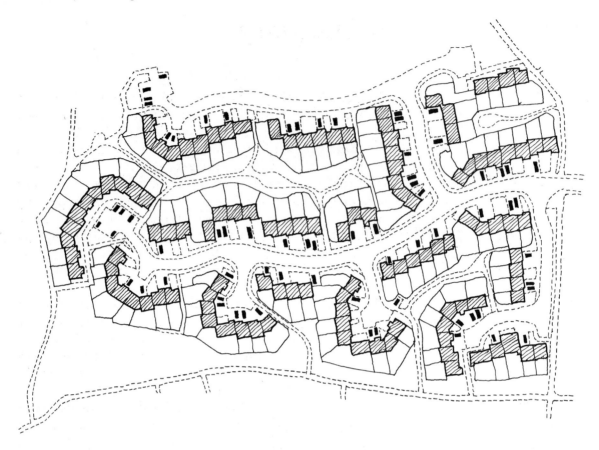

Figure 5.6 Part of area 31 showing that the road system is a cul-de-sac but that the footways form part of a complex through-network. All car parking is on hardstandings in front of the houses and there are no garages. There was no theft of cars from this area but the theft of property from cars was quite serious. (Source: Ordnance Survey (adapted).)

(*Figure 5.6*). Wherever these paths pass through or alongside a housing area, there is a tendency for more theft from cars to occur. What it appears to tell us is that housing areas which are designed to facilitate youths wandering through in an apparently legitimate manner are more likely to suffer this kind of theft. Where a housing area is not used as a through pedestrian route, it is much better protected.

The conclusion from both of these distributions of car crime suggests that housing with driveways and hardstandings in front of houses will have relatively little theft of cars, particularly where houses face each other across the street. In the case of theft from cars, it is also necessary to avoid creating pedestrian routes through groups of houses which can be used frequently by potential thieves living in nearby housing areas.

6 Burglary

Residential burglary is illegal entry into a house or flat usually for the purpose of stealing. In English law it is not necessary for a break-in or forcible entry to be involved but this is often the case. It can vary a great deal from a well-planned break-in to take valuable furniture, pictures, silverware or jewellery to incidents where the owner has found evidence of someone entering the property but where nothing was apparently taken. In Maguire's study of burglary, he attempted to classify the different types of burglary typical of different areas, from the country-house burglary in which more valuable items might be taken and burglaries in a wealthy suburb (his study included data on Gerrards Cross in Buckinghamshire) to more typical urban burglary in which television sets, videos and stereos and other similar electrical goods would be stolen. At the bottom end of the scale was the kind of burglary common on poor council estates which might involve the loss of small amounts of cash or the breaking into of coin meters (Maguire, 1982).

In an attempt to develop a useful classification of residential burglary for this research, we decided to separate flat burglaries from house burglaries (*Table 6.1*). We also separated burglaries involving break-ins to coin meters, and, as it is often difficult to distinguish between the two kinds of crime, brought this group together with those meter thefts classified by the police as theft. It also seems sensible to treat crime involving coin meters as a separate kind of problem from burglary. It is likely that the solution to this sort of crime will be found by replacing coin meters with alternative methods of payment, or by introducing pre-payment token meters (see Hill, 1986).

If we leave aside the thefts from coin meters, the principal groupings of burglary are into the different types of goods stolen. The idea behind this is that each type of stolen goods probably attracts different kinds of burglar or different methods of working. Taking luxury goods seemed likely to require some special knowledge of the value or means of selling or 'fencing' goods such as silverware, furs, china, porcelain, oriental carpets and clocks. Electrical goods such as televisions, videos and stereos would need a rather different and perhaps less organized network, but like luxury goods the thieves would require transport to remove the goods. The

TABLE 6.1 A classification of residential burglary in Harrow and Northampton with data from 1982

Crime type	Harrow per 10 000 households (N=367)	Northampton per 10 000 households (N=140)
House burglary		
Luxury goods	23	–
Electrical goods	61	40
Cash and jewellery	66	47
Trivial	8	10
Aggravated burglary	1	–
Burglary involving major damage	2	2
Unsuccessful attempts	47	53
Other	2	4
	210	156
Flat burglary	5	9
Coin meters		
Associated with a break-in	1	14
No signs of forced entry to dwelling	4	67
	5	81

(Source: Poyner, Helson and Webb, 1986)

third category, cash and jewellery, seemed to require the least organization for fencing goods and, as the items were so much more portable, it is less likely that such burglars would need a car or van to be parked nearby. They would also be more mobile in terms of escape routes, and might be prepared to take more risks since they would always be ready to run off in an emergency without leaving their spoils behind.

An unexpectedly large category of 'unsuccessful' burglaries emerged from this classification. These were incidents in which burglars appear to have been disturbed while attempting to break in, or they failed to break in for some reason, or if they did make an entry, they found nothing of value to them. Some of the cases where the offender did not break in would have been recorded by the police as criminal damage, but being less constrained than the police, we included them as attempts if this seemed the most likely explanation of the reported incident.

It is perhaps reassuring to note that two categories that are often portrayed in news reports and fictional accounts of crime are mercifully rare. The first is the stereotype of burglary that involves ransacking and damaging the home of the victim. Although there may be some damage to a window or door as part of gaining access, it is rare for any serious damage to be done inside. Indeed, we recall in one police file that there was a case of false reporting of a burglary by a woman who had tried to make a false claim against insurance. The main reason why the police became suspicious was that someone had gone to unusual lengths to make the house look a mess, including pouring the contents of a sauce bottle over a mattress and even unwrapping contraceptives and tying them in knots. The second category is the use of violence. It is rare for burglars to confront victims and use violence; more typically they run off if disturbed or pretend to be acting legitimately. Unfortunately, when aggravated burglaries do occur it is often elderly people who are the victims, hence the publicity for such unfortunate but rare incidents.

It is not our intention to describe the phenomenon of burglary in any great detail. For this, it would be better to turn to the research writings of those who have interviewed the offenders and their victims. The main references would be Mike Maguire's and Trevor Bennett's work in the Thames Valley area (Maguire, 1982) and Bennett's further work with Richard Wright on interviews with incarcerated burglars (Bennett and Wright, 1984). For earlier UK, Canadian and US research studies see Scarr (1973), Reppetto (1974), Waller and Okihiro (1978) and Walsh (1980).

Although there is a substantial literature on domestic burglary, we would suggest caution in assuming that most things are known about burglars and their motivation. The truth is that these studies are only based on a small proportion of offenders – those who get caught. Perhaps these are the less skilled, habitual offenders. The more skilful or less habitual offenders may be rarely caught. In our first study, of the 39 luxury goods burglaries none of the offenders was caught, although in three incidents the offenders were disturbed or seen running off (all men). One was seen at the top of a ladder by children already awake inside at 6.50 a.m. In the two main categories the offenders were arrested in only seven of the 125 electrical goods burglaries and eight of the 138 cash and jewellery burglaries (under 6%). All burglars who were caught lived locally and were male and so in social science jargon it may be a very unrepresentative sample. It is interesting to note that the higher value burglaries were not solved by the police.

Approaches to prevention

Before discussing the effect of different housing layouts on the various types of burglary, it is worth summarizing some of the conclusions that other researchers have arrived at. Although the more traditional response to burglary prevention has been the use of improved security in the form of better locks on doors and the introduction of locking devices on windows, the conclusion of all the researchers is that security is rather less important than other factors. It is suggested by Winchester and Jackson (1982) and Bennett and Wright (1984) that the more important factors which affect the choice of a target for burglary are those that can be recognized at a distance. Winchester and Jackson found that environmental risk factors were the most important determinant of burglary targets followed by occupancy rates and reward. Security levels contributed nothing to the selection of the target. Bennett and Wright appear to confirm this finding from their interviews with burglars. They found that 'surveillability' and 'occupancy' were the most important factors. Surveillance would be determined by the extent to which houses were overlooked by neighbours or passers-by and the ease with which access could be gained to the back of the house. Signs of occupancy might include a car being parked on the driveway or lights or noise coming from inside.

A further point in this theory is that burglars are unlikely to know with any certainty what security devices they might encounter until they attempted to break in. Typically, having selected a target house, a burglar might call at the front door to see if anyone would answer. If someone was home he could easily pass himself off as a legitimate caller. If no one came to the door and there was no other sign of life, such as a dog barking, the intending burglar would assume that he could try to make an entry through whatever way seemed easiest. Typically he might try the back of the house where windows or doors are least likely to be overlooked, but much would depend on the circumstances and whether it was light or dark, etc. It would only be at this point that the burglar would discover how secure windows and doors were. Most self-respecting burglars interviewed by researchers claimed that they could deal with almost any locks, by forcing if necessary.

There is less agreement on the value of the automatic burglar alarm in reducing the risk of burglary. Winchester and Jackson (1982) found that victimized houses were more likely to have an alarm. However, many of the convicted burglars interviewed by Bennett and Wright (1984) said that they were deterred by alarms, and these researchers cite Reppetto coming to a similar conclusion in his Boston study (Reppetto, 1974). There is also some evidence that burglaries of houses with alarms result in less being stolen (Conklin and Bittner, 1973; Winchester and Jackson, 1982).

Although there seems insufficient published research on how far alarms reduce the risk of domestic burglary, there are other problems with alarms which do seem to call their value into question. It is clear that the police usually have to deal with a very high proportion of false alarms. Apart from often wasting police time, alarm bells can also be very annoying to ordinary citizens trying to go about their normal business. In the end the question of alarms may be one of social values. Do we really want residential areas bristling with automatic alarm systems, or would we prefer to find other more subtle ways of dealing with the problem?

1987 Data

Crime data from the police computer for 1987 for the study area of north-east Northampton produced the statistics on burglary shown in *Table 6.2*. Some information was incomplete and hence some incidents could not be classified by the type of items stolen.

The first point to make about these figures is that they cannot be directly compared with the 1982 figures for Northampton (*Table 6.1*), because they are derived from a much smaller geographical area. However, whatever the differences in the geography, the crime rates for 1987 are considerably higher than for 1982 – more than double in most categories. The figures show that burglary in this part of Northampton is at least as bad as those described as 'medium-risk areas' in British Crime Survey findings (Hough and Mayhew, 1985) and certainly as bad as some inner-city problem estates that we have studied.

The one exception to these increases is the thefts from coin meters which are not associated with a break-in. On the face of it this is an encouraging reduction, but we do not know if there is a reason such as the gradual removal or replacement of these meters. The more likely explanation is that the north-east Northampton study area does not include the old streets of terraced houses which may well house the greater proportion of these meters and which were included in the Northampton data in *Table 6.1*.

TABLE 6.2 Residential burglary in north-east Northampton, 1987

Crime type	Number of crimes	Rate per 10 000 households
House burglary		
Luxury goods	8	6
Electrical goods	238	170
Cash and jewellery	103	74
Trivial	8	6
Aggravated burglary	2	1
Burglary involving major damage	1	1
Unsuccessful attempts	148	106
Other	10	7
Not yet known what was stolen	32	22
	550	393
Flats and residential institutions	14	10
Coin meters		
Associated with a break-in	19	14
No signs of forced entry to dwelling	25	18
	44	32
Total residential burglary	608	435

The figures confirm the importance of the two main categories of burglary of electrical goods and cash and jewellery, and these categories will be discussed in more detail below. However, before doing so it might be interesting to consider the special nature of the distribution of luxury goods. Even with a much larger sample of crime reports it still does not emerge as a significant problem in the north-east Northampton study area. In Harrow in the 1982 data it was not a very large category, but when plotted on a map of the Harrow study area, a very distinct distribution emerged (*Figure 6.1*).

As can be seen from *Figure 6.1*, the spot map shows the 39 burglaries concentrated in the two areas which are very up-market housing. A more detailed examination of these incidents reveals that the distribution is even more confined to these areas if the borderline cases in the classification are removed, that is burglaries with only a mention of one or two luxury items among several other stolen items. It might be argued that this kind of up-market housing should be treated as a special high-risk case and be more highly protected because of its attractiveness as a target for burglary, and some

Figure 6.1 The distribution of luxury goods burglary in Harrow, 1982.

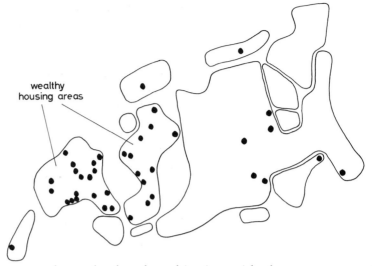

owners have clearly taken this view with alarm systems and even electrically operated gates and highwalls around the perimeter of their property (*Figure 6.2*). However, as the map in *Figure 3.1* showed, the houses are laid out in a way which must make them particularly vulnerable to burglary. There is ample cover from mature foliage and walls, it is easy to gain access to the rear of the property and the backs of many gardens face on to open land. Perhaps developers should give careful thought to the design of such wealthy enclaves so that they do not present such inviting targets. Whatever the conclusion, it is perhaps fair to say that this is not the main problem for crime prevention. If we do want to dramatically reduce residential burglary, our efforts should be directed at the more mainstream problems of burglary from middle and lower income housing.

Figure 6.2 This photograph illustrates the high level of perimeter security adopted by some to protect their homes in Stanmore, an area that suffers from the relatively unusual problem of burglary of luxury goods such as paintings, furs, silverware, porcelain, and oriental rugs.

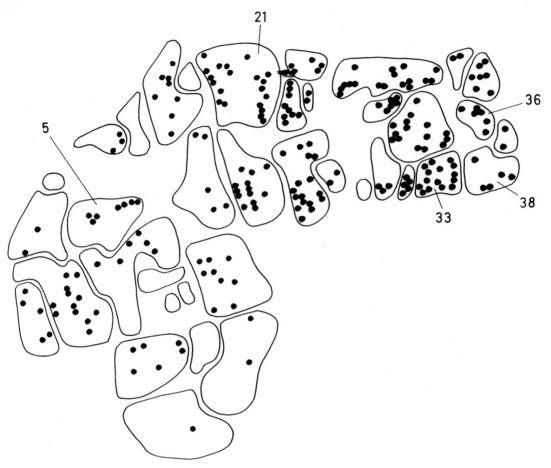

Figure 6.3 The distribution of electrical goods burglary in north-east Northampton, 1987.

Mainstream burglary

There are only two large groups of crime in the Northampton study area that are suitable for more detailed analysis. These are electrical goods burglary and cash and jewellery burglary. It is true that in *Table 6.2* the category of unsuccessful burglaries is of a similar size, but this group is by definition one in which we have poor information. We do not know what the objectives of these burglaries were and we do not know why they failed. It may be that the offenders were disturbed or that the security arrangements were too good for them, or again they may not have found what they were looking for. For these reasons we have not made any further analysis, even though a study of a much larger sample of failures might prove very interesting.

The two maps of burglary in north-east Northampton raise a number of questions (*Figures 6.3* and *6.4*). The first is that our theory about the two kinds of burglary being different in nature does seem to be supported by the two crime

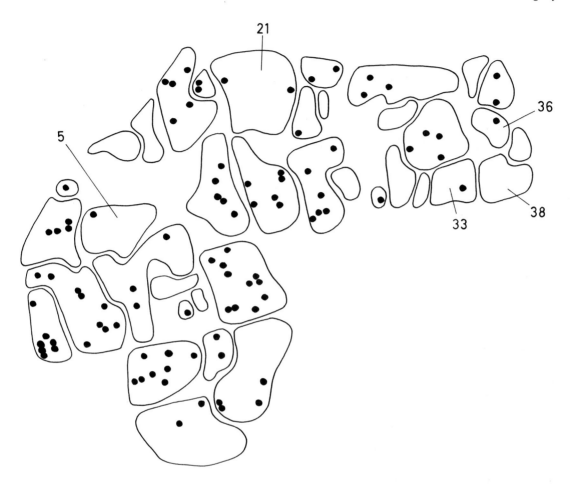

Figure 6.4 The distribution of cash and jewellery burglary in north-east Northampton, 1987.

distributions. Although the locations for these two kinds of crime are fairly well distributed across the map, it is also possible to find areas which have concentrations of electrical goods burglary but little or no cash and jewellery burglary. Examples of this are areas 5, 21, 33, 36 and 38.

When we began to develop our analysis of these two distributions we realized that if we worked out the crime rates for each area and placed them in order of seriousness, the two ranking lists were very different. To illustrate this visually, *Figure 6.5* shows two maps of the study area, one with the ten areas with the highest crime rates for electrical goods and the other with the ten areas with the highest rates of cash and jewellery burglary. The pattern of shaded areas on the two maps is very different. Electrical goods tend to be stolen in the areas of newer housing at the eastern end of the study area furthest away from the town centre, whereas the cash and jewellery burglaries tend to be closer to the town centre in a variety of older types of housing.

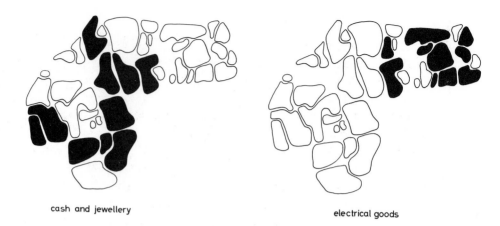

cash and jewellery　　　　　　　　electrical goods

Figure 6.5 Contrasting distributions of the ten worst areas for electrical goods burglary and for cash and jewellery burglary.

In trying to understand what design and layout factors of these areas might explain these differences, we were aware of the factors which had been put forward by previous researchers such as Winchester and Jackson (1982) and others summarized in Poyner (1983). Further ideas have been put forward by Alice Coleman in an article in *House Builder* (Coleman, 1987) which focuses on the importance of traditional design relationships of houses facing the street with waist-high front and side fences and enclosed back gardens with access only from the street and not through a back gate. We were also influenced by the variety of housing forms in the area of Northampton we had chosen to study. Each of the areas was different in design and layout, representing a wide range of styles and periods of housing since the 1914–18 war, including modern public and private sector housing.

From this familiarity with other literature and our own observations of the area, we set about defining a number of design factors which might explain the two distributions. A good deal of time was spent trying out various definitions and combinations and in the end we arrived at the following likely candidates.

Accessibility
– number of roads connecting the area to other areas;
– the existence of through streets carrying traffic through the area;
– through pedestrian routes, not available to vehicles.

Older houses
– houses built between 1918 and 1939.

Surveillance
- roadway access to housing being overlooked by the houses it serves;
- windows facing each other across the road/street;
- medium-depth front gardens (Coleman, 1987, suggests 3–5 m depth);
- foliage in front gardens (particularly evergreen trees and shrubs);
- front door facing street.

Vulnerability
- low walls around front garden;
- open access at side of house to back garden;
- paths at the back with gate into back garden;
- deep mature back gardens;
- high fences or walls around back garden/yard;
- open land behind houses.

Escape routes
- escape routes by foot to safe places (such as open ground or a maze of footpaths);
- short footpath escape routes to places where cars can be left without suspicion.

Other
- public sector housing;
- distance from town centre.

Analyses of these factors for both kinds of burglary are presented in *Tables 6.3* and *6.4*. In each case the crime rates have been calculated for each of the housing areas with 100 or more houses and arranged in order of seriousness for both crimes, from crime free areas down to those with the most crimes areas. The rank order is considerably different for the two categories. Against each area is an analysis of the characteristics of the housing design and layout. Inevitably this is a generalization but since the housing design and layout are usually fairly uniform across each area, a general analysis can be made. To aid presentation, the 31 areas are divided into three levels, the ten lowest crime rates and the ten highest at the top and bottom of each table, respectively. The tables may take some time to digest but they do reveal that the two kinds of burglary are controlled by a different pattern of environmental factors.

TABLE 6.3 An analysis of the environmental factors influencing electrical goods burglary

				Accessibility				Surveillance					Vulnerability						P Escape	
Area	Rate	PubS	D/T	Rds 4s	Rds	Ped	Old house	Road-ways	Win-dows	Frnt 3–5 m	Folg	Door face	Wall frnt	Side acc.	Back gate	Back open	Deep grdn	Fence back	Safe area	Car park
7	0	●●●	●	–	••	–	–	•••	•••	•••	–	•••	●●●	–	–	–	–	••	–	–
13	0	–	●	–	•••	–	•••	•••	•••	•••	•	••	●●	●	–	–	–	•••	•••	–
16	0	–	●	–	–	–	–	•••	•••	•••	–	–	●●●	–	–	–	–	•••	–	–
12	2	–	●	–	–	–	–	•••	•••	•••	–	–	–	–	–	–	–	•••	–	–
3	3	–	–	•••	•••	–	•••	•••	•••	•••	–	•••	●●●	–	•	–	•	•••	–	–
6	6	–	●	•••	•••	–	•••	•••	•••	•••	•	•••	●●●	–	•	–	••	•••	–	–
14	8	–	●	–	–	•••	–	•••	•••	•••	••	•	●	••	–	–	•••	•••	•••	–
5	9	●●●	●	••	•	–	–	•••	•••	•••	–	–	●●●	–	–	–	–	•	–	–
15	9	●●●	●	–	–	–	–	•••	•••	–	–	••	–	–	•••	–	–	•••	•••	–
31	9	●●●	●●●	–	–	•••	–	•••	•••	–	–	•••	–	–	•••	•	–	•••	•••	•••
34	11	–	●●●	–	–	–	–	•••	•••	•••	–	•••	●●●	–	–	–	–	•••	•••	•••
2	12	●●●	–	•••	•••	–	•••	•••	•••	•••	–	•••	●●	●●●	–	–	–	–	–	–
1	13	–	–	•••	•••	–	•••	•••	•••	–	–	•••	●●●	–	•••	–	•••	•••	•••	–
19	13	–	●	–	–	•••	–	•••	•••	•••	–	•••	–	–	•	–	–	•••	•••	–
10	14	–	●	–	–	••	••	•••	•••	•••	••	•	●●●	●●●	–	•	••	•••	•••	•••
21	17	●●●	●●	•	•••	•••	–	–	–	–	–	–	–	–	•••	–	–	•••	•••	•••
17	19	–	●	•	•••	–	•••	•••	•••	•••	•	–	●●●	●	•	–	•••	•••	–	–
26	19	–	●●	–	•••	•••	–	•••	•••	•••	–	•••	–	–	•••	–	–	•••	•••	•••
11	20	–	●	••	•	–	•••	•••	•••	•••	•••	••	●●●	●	–	••	•••	•••	•••	–
22	20	–	●●	–	–	–	–	•••	••	•••	–	••	–	●●	–	–	–	•••	•••	–
20	21	●●●	●●	–	–	•••	–	–	–	–	–	–	–	–	•••	–	–	•••	•••	•••
27	21	●●●	●●●	••	•••	•••	–	–	–	–	–	–	–	–	•••	••	–	•••	•••	•••
29	21	●●●	●●●	•••	–	•••	–	–	–	–	–	–	–	–	•••	–	–	•••	•••	•••
35	23	●●●	●●●	•	–	•••	–	–	–	–	••	–	–	–	•••	–	–	•••	•••	•••
25	23	●●●	●●	•	•••	•••	–	–	–	–	–	–	–	–	•••	–	–	•••	•••	•••
38	23	–	●●●	–	–	–	–	•	•	••	–	••	–	–	•••	••	–	•••	•••	–
36	24	–	●●●	•	–	•••	–	••	•	•••	–	•	–	●●●	–	–	–	•••	•••	•••
32	30	●●●	●●●	–	–	•••	–	–	–	–	–	–	–	–	•••	–	–	•••	•••	•••
28	33	–	●●●	–	–	•••	–	•	•	•••	–	•	–	●	–	–	–	•••	•••	•••
33	37	–	●●●	–	–	•••	–	••	••	•••	–	•	–	●●●	–	•	–	•	•••	•••
24	63	–	●●	–	–	•••	–	••	•	•••	–	••	–	–	•••	–	••	•••	•••

Area – The housing area number (only housing areas with more than 100 houses included).
Rate – Crime rate per 1000 households.
PubS – Public sector housing (denoted by ●●●).
D/T – Distance from town centre.

Accessibility
Rds/4s – Road entrances into the area from other areas (one ● per four intersections).
Rds – The extent of through roads in the area, carrying traffic through it.
Ped – Pedestrian through routes which are separate from the roads.

Old house – Old houses built between 1918 and 1939.

Surveillance
Roadways – Roadway access to housing overlooked by the houses it serves.
Windows – House windows face each other across the street.
Frnt 3–5 m – The depth of front gardens.
Folg – The extent of foliage in front gardens such as mature trees and shrubs.
Door face – Front doors face the street.

Vulnerability
Wall frnt – Low walls around front garden.
Side acc. – Open access at side of house to rear garden.
Back gate – Houses with a path at the bottom of the back garden and a back garden gate.
Back open – Open land at the back of houses.
Deep grdn – Houses which have deep mature back gardens.
Fence back – High fences or walls around back garden/yard.

P Escape
Safe area – Escape routes by foot to safe places, such as open ground or a maze of footpaths.
Car park – Short footpath escape routes to places where cars can be parked without suspicion.

TABLE 6.4 An analysis of the environmental factors influencing cash and jewellery burglary

Area	Rate	PubS	D/T	Accessibility			Old house	Surveillance					Vulnerability						P Escape	
				Rds 4s	Rds	Ped		Road-ways	Win-dows	Frnt 3–5 m	Folg	Door face	Wall frnt	Side acc.	Back gate	Back open	Deep grdn	Fence back	Safe area	Car park
7	0	●●●	●	–	●●	–	–	●●●	●●●	●●●	–	●●●	●●●	–	–	–	–	●●	–	–
15	0	●●●	●	–	●●	–	–	●●●	●●●	–	–	●●	–	–	●●●	–	–	●●●	●●●	–
16	0	–	●	–	–	–	–	●●●	●●●	●●●	–	–	–	–	–	–	–	●●●	–	–
26	0	–	●●	–	●●●	●●●	–	●●●	●●●	●●●	–	●●●	–	–	–	–	–	●●●	●●●	●●●
28	0	–	●●●	–	–	●●●	–	●	●	●●●	●	●	–	●	–	–	–	●●●	●●●	●●●
31	0	●●●	●●●	–	–	●●●	–	●●●	●●●	–	–	●●●	–	–	●●●	●	–	●	●●●	●●●
32	0	●●●	●●●	–	–	●●●	–	–	–	–	–	–	–	–	●●●	–	–	●●●	●●●	●●●
34	0	–	●●●	–	–	–	–	●●●	●●●	●●●	–	●●●	●●●	–	–	–	–	●●●	●●●	●●●
38	0	–	●●●	–	–	–	–	●	●	●●	●	●●	–	–	–	–	–	●●	●●●	–
5	1	●●●	●	●●	●●●	–	–	●●●	●●●	●●●	–	●●●	●●●	–	●●	–	–	●	–	–
21	2	●●●	●●	●	●●●	●●●	–	–	–	–	–	–	–	–	●●●	–	–	●●●	●●●	●●●
33	2	–	●●●	–	–	●●●	–	●●	●●	●●●	–	●	–	●●●	–	●	–	●	●●●	●●●
6	3	–	●	●●●	●●●	–	●●●	●●●	●●●	●●●	●	●●●	●●●	–	●	–	●●	●●●	–	–
27	4	●●●	●●●	●●	●●●	●●●	–	–	–	–	–	–	–	–	●●●	●●	–	●●●	●●●	●●●
36	4	–	●●●	●	–	●●●	–	●●	●	●●●	–	●	–	●●●	–	–	–	●●●	●●●	●●●
12	5	–	●	–	–	–	–	●●●	●●●	●●●	–	●●●	–	–	–	–	–	●●●	●●●	–
3	6	–	–	●●●	●●●	–	●●●	●●●	●●●	●●●	–	●●●	–	–	●	–	●	●●●	●●●	–
29	6	●●●	●●●	●●●	–	–	–	–	–	–	–	–	–	–	●●●	–	–	●●●	●●●	●●●
24	7	–	●●	–	–	●●●	–	●●	●	●●●	–	●●	–	–	●●●	–	–	●●	●●●	●●●
35	7	●●●	●●●	●	–	●●●	–	–	–	–	●●	–	–	–	●●●	–	–	●●●	●●●	●●●
22	8	–	●●	–	–	–	–	●●●	●●	●●●	–	●●	–	–	●●	–	–	●●●	●●●	–
25	8	●●●	●●	●	●●●	●●●	–	–	–	–	–	–	–	–	●●●	–	–	●●●	●●●	●●●
2	9	●●●	–	●●●	●●●	–	●●●	●●●	●●●	●●●	–	●●●	●●	●●●	–	–	–	–	●●●	–
20	10	●●●	●●	–	–	●●●	–	–	–	–	–	–	–	–	●●●	–	–	●●●	●●●	●●●
17	12	–	●	●	●●●	–	●●●	●●●	●●●	●●●	●●●	●	●●●	●●●	●	–	●●●	●●●	–	–
19	13	–	●	–	–	●●●	–	●●●	●●●	●●●	–	●●●	–	●	–	–	–	●●●	●●●	–
13	16	–	●	–	●●●	–	●●●	●●●	●●●	●●	–	●●	●●	–	●	–	–	●●●	●●●	–
14	16	–	●	–	–	●●●	–	●●●	●●●	–	●●	–	–	●	–	–	●●●	●●●	●●●	–
10	17	–	●	–	–	●●	●●	●●●	●●●	●●●	●●	●	●●●	●●●	–	–	●●	●●●	●●●	–
1	18	–	–	●●●	●●●	–	●●●	●●●	●●●	–	–	●●●	●●●	–	●●●	–	●●●	●●●	●●●	–
11	27	–	●	●●	–	–	●●●	●●●	●●●	●●●	●●●	●●	●●●	●●	–	●●	●●●	●●●	●●●	–

Area – The housing area number (only housing areas with more than 100 houses included).
Rate – Crime rate per 1000 households.
PubS – Public sector housing (denoted by ●●●).
D/T – Distance from town centre.

Accessibility
Rds/4s – Road entrances into the area from other areas (one ● per four intersections).
Rds – The extent of through roads in the area, carrying traffic through it.
Ped – Pedestrian through routes which are separate from the roads.

Old house – Old houses built between 1918 and 1939.

Surveillance
Roadways – Roadway access to housing overlooked by the houses it serves.
Windows – House windows face each other across the street.
Frnt 3–5 m – The depth of front gardens.
Folg – The extent of foliage in front gardens such as mature trees and shrubs.
Door face – Front doors face the street.

Vulnerability
Wall frnt – Low walls around front garden.
Side acc. – Open access at side of house to rear garden.
Back gate – Houses with a path at the bottom of the back garden and a back garden gate.
Back open – Open land at the back of houses.
Deep grdn – Houses which have deep mature back gardens.
Fence back – High fences or walls around back garden/yard.

P Escape
Safe area – Escape routes by foot to safe places, such as open ground or a maze of footpaths.
Car park – Short footpath escape routes to places where cars can be parked without suspicion.

Electrical goods burglary

The analysis in *Table 6.3* shows that many of the environmental factors differ between low- and high-crime areas. Burglary of electrical goods tends to occur in the following kinds of housing area:

new housing further from the town centre;
where there are pedestrian through routes;
where there is a lack of surveillance of roadways;
where houses do not face each other (front doors and windows);
where there are back garden gates off footpaths;
where there are pedestrian escape routes to car parking;
there is also some evidence to suggest that open-plan fronts are more vulnerable.

It seems clear from the data in *Table 6.3* that if these characteristics of housing areas are removed the opportunity for this kind of burglary is reduced and less burglary of this kind will occur. In practical terms what appears necessary from inspection of the above list is that surveillance should be maximized by making houses face each other across the street and overlook the access roads. Efforts should also be made to avoid footpaths which create through pedestrian routes and provide foot-only escape routes to places where cars can be left ready for a get-away (*Figure 6.6*). It appears that a back gate should be avoided and a low wall around the front garden also seems to help discourage this kind of burglary. Perhaps this helps to make an offender more obvious when leaving the premises carrying more bulky electrical goods.

Figure 6.6(a, b) The design of this sort of housing in area 24 provides plenty of opportunity for electrical goods burglary. The maze of paths throughout the area gives easy access to rear gardens and also facilitates escape to nearby areas where cars can be parked unnoticed.

(a)

(b)

Cash and jewellery burglary

The design characteristics which favour cash and jewellery burglaries are significantly different from those which favour the burglary of electrical goods. A careful study of *Table 6.4* shows that cash and jewellery burglaries are less related to the car and tend to occur in the following types of housing settings:

housing which is nearer the town centre;
housing areas with more road access points;
older houses;
the presence of foliage at the front and long back gardens seem to assist the offender;
open side access to the rear is more important than back gates;
escape routes on foot are useful but not to reach a parked car.

The relevance of these factors is easy to understand. Unlike electrical goods burglary, cash and jewellery burglary is done on foot and housing nearer to the town centre may be more accessible to potential criminals. The street pattern is more accessible and strangers walking these streets will not arouse suspicion. If a target is selected and the intending burglar calls at the front door, foliage and an enclosed front garden will give some cover (*Figure 6.7*). If he finds no one at home, open access around the side of the house to a secluded back garden is ideal for this kind of crime. It is also possible that older houses are seen as easier to burgle because they may have less sound window frames and doors, and perhaps the older locking hardware is broken or well worn. Perhaps also older

Figure 6.7 The foliage in front of these mature houses in area 11 gives good cover and benefits cash and jewellery burglary.

houses have more nooks and crannies and provide better picking for old jewellery and keepsakes, etc., compared with the life style of the new town houses with their videos and stereos.

This form of burglary seems to be much more speculative or opportunistic, and from this analysis we can claim that housing designed with limited road access, relatively open fronts and with no easy access to the rear will have little burglary of this kind.

Although the two kinds of mainstream burglary have rather different implications for design, they do not generally conflict. However, there does seem to be some conflict on the question of low front garden walls. There are moderate correlations with crime and front walls which suggest that there is less electrical goods burglary when walls are present but more risk of cash and jewellery. There are at least two ways of looking at these findings. It could be said that the correlations are little more than coincidence because newer housing suffers more from electrical goods burglary but tends not to have front walls whereas older housing which suffers more from cash and jewellery burglary tends to have front walls.

Perhaps a more precise view of these findings is that front walls may have some value in defining the front garden area or territory of a house and thereby make an intruder more conspicuous, particularly when carrying stolen property. However, the wall may also encourage the development of mature foliage around a property which then has the opposite effect of providing some cover and reducing surveillance by neighbours. Our conclusion must be that walls or fences around the front of a house can be both beneficial and a disadvantage, and so in Chapter 11 where design requirements are summarized we have not recommended them as important to burglary prevention.

7 Theft from garages

There is a distinct group of crimes associated with domestic garages. From the 1987 Northampton data we identified 59 thefts from garages. Although this amounts to only 2.5% of residential crime in the study area and four thefts per 1000 households, the problem does relate strongly to design and layout.

No conventional crime statistics would reveal these crimes because they are officially classified under other headings. The commonest items stolen from domestic garages are bicycles; sometimes two or even three are taken at the same time. These are recorded in Home Office statistics as bicycle thefts even if the garage was forcibly opened by the thieves. Most of the remaining thefts from garages were classified as 'other theft', even when entry was gained only by forcing locks or doors. Occasionally thefts from garages are recorded as burglaries.

Very little can be said about the offenders for these crimes because few are ever caught. From our earlier study of residential crime in Northampton and Harrow, out of 62 thefts from garages and sheds, the offenders had been caught in only two cases. This theft from garages seems to be an explorative form of behaviour. Prospective thieves seem to search an area in the hope of finding material in garages worth stealing. Apart from bicycles, the material stolen from garages included a bewildering array of power tools, gardening tools and particularly power mowers, food from freezer cabinets and sports equipment, and it is easy to see why garages can provide an attractive target.

By the nature of the location it may be some time before a garage theft is discovered. The crime reports suggest that there is a tendency for these thefts to occur in the evening and over the weekend, but this may be when householders are most likely to discover their losses. Most of the thefts from garages do not seem to involve the forcing of locks or doors. Police records do not always say whether the garage was properly secured or not, but in 20% of the crimes it was recorded that force was used to gain entry. Certainly we know from observation of any residential area that it is easy to come across houses with garage doors left open, particularly at the weekend, and it is easy to believe that many side and back doors of garages will also be left unlocked.

There is further evidence of the explorative nature of this criminal behaviour recorded under 'criminal damage'. Some of these crimes involve damage to garage doors and padlocks, which suggests that intending thieves broke in but found nothing worth stealing.

The security option

When crime prevention specialists are faced with the question of how to reduce theft from garages, they will recommend the use of extra locks. The British Standard Guide for *Security of buildings against crime* (1986) illustrates this approach on p.36 by recommending, for an up and over garage door, either a stout padlock or two mortice locks in addition to the one supplied with the door. Although this may sound like a sensible security measure, it does not really meet many of the problems behind the crime reports. In the crime reports either the doors were not locked or the locks such as padlocks were forced or broken open. Having more locks does not seem to help. It discourages the use of the locks because users will need two keys and they will have to go to the extra trouble of locking and unlocking two or three locks every time they go to the garage. It is an obvious inconvenience compared with the single lock solution.

Layout design critical

In our earlier study of Harrow, for which we have much more detailed police reports, the locations of many of the crimes were visited and documented. We were interested to find out whether or not the location of the garage would have an impact on the risk of crime. Observations of run-down estates often reveal damaged and graffiti-covered garage doors when they are arranged in blocks away from houses or flats, whereas garages placed alongside houses seemed to be much less damaged. Could this be the case for these crimes of theft?

It was easy to separate garages which were built on the side of the house facing the street from those built at the end of the garden facing a side street or some back alley or yard. *Table 7.1* shows the data for 33 garage thefts in which we have clear descriptions of the security of the garage and whether or not force was used to gain entry.

Simple figures such as these offer a powerful argument to support the case that the location of the garage has a major effect on its security. The only garages to be broken into were

Theft from garages 63

TABLE 7.1 Thefts from garages in Harrow with different security and in different locations

State of security	Garages at side of house with access at the front	Garages away from the house
Locked garages	0	7
Unlocked garages	21	5

(Source: Poyner, Helson and Webb, 1985)

those built away from the house, at the end of the garden or in a separate garage block. Most thefts were from garages at the side of houses, but none of these thefts involved forced entry. What this data appears to suggest is that thefts from garages at the side of the house only occur when the doors are left unlocked or open. There is no evidence that suggests anything but minimum security is required for garages at the side of the house (presumably some simple lock, as is already fitted as standard to most up and over doors).

For garages away from the house the problem is quite different. Here there is a good change of a break-in taking place. It does not seem to make much difference how the garage is locked up. Provided the door is away from the house in a secluded or remote position, intending thieves can usually find a way of breaking the locks or finding some other means of entry. Although few in number, it is clear from the descriptions of garage break-ins that quite substantial force was sometimes used, including breaking padlocks and levering off locking devices.

What seems important here is the potential surveillance of garages at the side of the house, by residents themselves, by neighbours and by people in the houses opposite. Exceptions often prove rules and it was noted in the first study that the only garage located at the side of the house to be broken into was in Northampton. This house was in a secluded area at the end of a cul-de-sac, not overlooked by other houses and with a public footpath running along the side of the garage. The property had been up for sale for several months and it was believed that no one was living in it at the time of the break-in.

The conclusion from this analysis seems to provide a paradigm for the whole question of residential crime prevention. It illustrates the relative importance of layout design and security provision. Garages have to be locked up if they are to be secure. Open garage doors would be an obvious invitation to a thief, but as long as the garage is in a safe location in which it can be well supervised by the household or its neighbours on either side or opposite, then only quite modest security seems necessary. Of course no one can claim that a determined thief cannot break into the garage, but it does not seem to be worth the risk of being caught. The solution is a balance of security and surveillance which can only be created through design.

Although we do not have the exact addresses for crime locations in the 1987 data, the importance of garage location is soon confirmed when we map the thefts for 1987. There were 50 thefts which can be plotted on to the map (*Figure 7.1*) and we have also added the few criminal damage cases mentioned earlier. Although there are a few incidents in most of the housing areas, there are three or four main clusters of dots. In every case these small clusters are associated with garages in back alleyways or garage courts (*Figure 7.2*). No doubt some of the thefts occur in garages located at the side or on the front of the house (*Figure 7.3*), but these will probably be garages left insecure. Clearly, in addition to good layout, garages need to have easily operated and self-locking doors to encourage users to keep them locked.

Although there will be difficulties in providing garages in terraced housing, the preferred location for domestic garages is attached to or built alongside the house. The value of this is that such garages are unlikely to be broken into by force, and they will therefore only need to be locked when not in use to be free from crime. Garages in other situations will always be more at risk from break-in even if heavily secured.

Figure 7.2 Most thefts and particularly break-ins to garages are associated with locations where garages are remote from the houses they serve.

Figure 7.3 Garages which have this close relationship with the house need only a minimal amount of security to be free of crime.

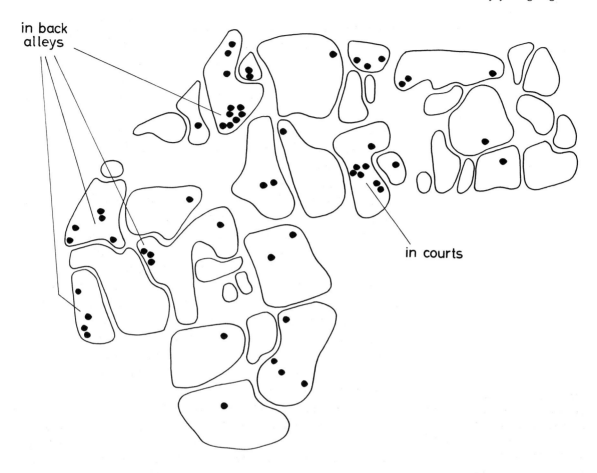

Figure 7.1 The distribution of thefts from garages in north-east Northampton, 1987.

8 Theft outside the house

In addition to the more commonly recognized crimes of burglary and autocrime, there is a good deal of other theft associated with the home which in the first study amounted to 8% of all crime in Northampton (see *Table 2.2*). These thefts can occur inside or outside the house. Those that occur inside may involve theft by friends or visitors to the household, including lodgers, relatives, babysitters, ex-lodgers and ex-live-in boyfriends. They may be thefts which occurred during a party or when builders and decorators were suspected. Another method of theft is by deception when, typically, two or more youths gain access to the house on some pretext, one distracting the occupant while the other searches for money. A further category which we included under residential crime was thefts which occur in residential institutions such as old peoples' homes.

These 'inside jobs' cannot be controlled by design and layout of housing because they are done by people who have been given access. However, where thefts occur outside the house but within its curtilage (about 18% of residential crime in Northampton), there do seem to be ways in which the design and layout of housing can provide more security. In the first study four categories of outside theft were identified – milk from doorsteps, clothes from washing lines, and plants and ornaments and bicycles from front and back gardens. With the help of the larger sample of 1987 crime data, we found further categories and decided to include thefts from sheds. This produced the groups of thefts outside the house shown in *Table 8.1*.

Most of these categories of theft are too small to produce separate map distributions sufficient to be analysed in the manner of previous chapters. However, it did seem worth examining the distribution of all theft outside the house taken together. In developing this analysis we recognized that the theft of motorcycles seemed to have much in common with the theft of bicycles, as motorcycles are also left about in much the same places such as front and back gardens and so this category of theft has been included in the analysis.

The map in *Figure 8.1* shows the crimes outside the house (including motorcycle thefts) which could be plotted within the housing areas. As the distribution shows there are a

TABLE 8.1 Theft outside the house in north-east Northampton, 1987

Crime type	N	Rate per 10 000 households
Plants and garden ornaments stolen	17	12
Items taken from doorsteps (milk, parcels, etc.)	25	18
Property taken from external meter boxes	7	5
Theft of pedal cycles (gardens and driveways)	56	40
Clothes from washing lines	25	18
Thefts from garden sheds	36	26
Other thefts from outside	27	19
Total	193	138

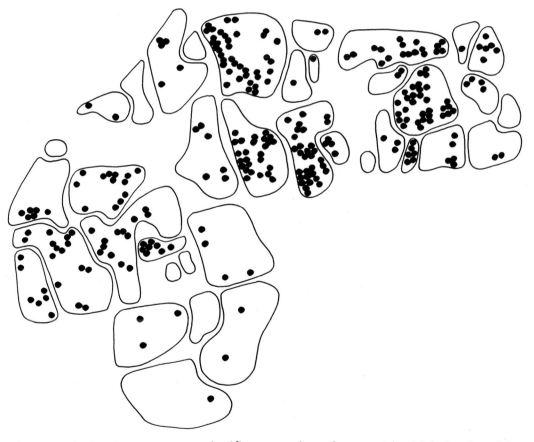

Figure 8.1 The distribution of thefts from outside the house in north-east Northampton, 1987.

significant number of areas with a high density of these crimes and a significant number with few crimes. There is a marked pattern of high crime rates on public sector housing, but the more analytic approach used here, in *Table 8.2*, will show that this is due more to the design characteristics of these areas than to the nature of their tenure. The main difficulty arises in terraced housing whether or not it is part of a public sector estate.

The map distribution in *Figure 8.1* is analysed in a tabular form as in previous chapters. The crime rate per 1000 households was calculated for each area and arranged in rank order as before from lowest to highest crime rate.

TABLE 8.2 An analysis of the environmental factors influencing theft from outside the home

Area	Rate per 1000 households	Public sector	Windows face	Small front garden	Low front walls	Back garden gate	High back fence	Terrace houses	Front gate to back	Garages
13	0	•	•••	•	••	–	•••	•	••	••
16	0	–	•••	–	–	–	•••	–	•••	•••
12	2	–	•••	–	–	–	•••	–	•••	•••
34	5	–	•••	–	•••	–	•••	–	•••	••
10	6	–	•••	–	•••	–	•••	–	••	•••
15	6	•••	•••	•	–	•••	•••	•••	–	••
24	7	–	••	–	–	–	••	–	•••	•••
14	8	–	•••	–	•	–	•••	–	•••	•••
22	8	–	••	–	–	–	•••	–	•••	•••
31	9	•••	•••	•	–	•••	•	•••	–	–
38	9	–	••	–	•	–	•••	–	•••	•••
3	10	–	•••	–	•••	•	•••	•••	–	•
11	10	–	•••	–	•••	–	•••	–	••	•
28	11	–	••	–	–	–	•••	–	•••	•••
17	12	–	•••	–	•••	•	•••	–	•••	•••
33	12	–	••	–	–	–	••	–	•••	•
2	14	•••	•••	–	•••	–	–	•••	•••	–
6	14	–	•••	–	•••	–	•••	–	•	•••
1	16	–	••	•••	•••	•••	•••	•••	•••	•••
5	16	•••	•••	•	•••	••	•	•••	–	•
19	16	–	••	–	–	•	•••	•	•	••
36	16	–	•	–	–	–	•••	–	•••	•••
27	23	•••	–	•••	–	•••	•••	•••	–	•
35	29	•••	–	•••	–	•••	•••	•••	–	–
21	33	•••	–	•••	–	•••	•••	•••	–	–
32	37	•••	–	•••	–	•••	•••	•••	–	–
7	38	•••	•••	–	•••	–	••	•••	–	•
26	38	–	•••	–	–	–	•••	–	–	•••
25	39	•••	–	•••	–	•••	•••	•••	–	–
20	42	•••	–	•••	–	•••	•••	•••	–	–
29	46	•••	–	•••	–	•••	•••	•••	–	–

Figure 8.2 Terraced housing, particularly with small front garden areas, tends to have more outside theft.

Figure 8.3 Back garden gates, particularly with slatted construction, encourage theft from back gardens.

The facts that seemed to explain the map distribution in *Figure 8.1* were as follows.

Terraced housing – Housing areas with a lot of outside theft are more likely to be predominantly built in terraces (*Figure 8.2*).

Front windows facing – Generally, where houses are not planned facing other houses across the street or in a similar relationship, there is more theft around the house. We assume this is due to a lack of mutual surveillance by neighbours.

Small front gardens – Houses with little distance between the front face of the house and the road or pathway have more theft. It does not make much difference to have a low wall or fence at the front.

Back garden gate – There is more theft when back gates open onto parking courts or footpaths at the back of the house. The problem seems worst when the back path is a long through path and when the rear gate and/or fence has a slatted construction through which is is easy to see into the back garden and reach in to unbolt the gate (*Figure 8.3*).

Front gate to back garden – Theft is not serious where there is a side gate to the back garden or yard from the front of the house.

Garages – Where garages are provided there tends to be less theft around the house. This is probably because the garage is a relatively safe place to store tools, bicycles and motorcycles, garden furniture, etc.

This analysis of theft around the house gives only a general indication of how layout can reduce outside theft. Because there are several kinds of theft involved, it is necessary to break the problem of outside theft into several components.

A secure back yard

In the kind of low-rise housing we are considering there is usually some outside garden or yard area attached to the house. This outside area is generally provided to give privacy, adequate natural lighting and the amenity of a garden whether used ornamentally or for growing fruit and vegetables.

Because of the economic pressures to minimize the size of houses it is not possible to provide space for all the household's activities within the house. If some activities cannot be done inside the house because they take up a lot of space or because they are messy or dirty, then they will take place outside the house. Some storage and repair activities are often moved to the garage or garden shed such as freezer cabinets, tools, bicycles, motorcycles, prams and lawnmowers and garden furniture. However, if there is no garage or shed or these are inadequate for the demand, some items have to be stored outside. Judging by the police crime reports, the items which tend to be stolen are motorcycles, bicycles, lawnmowers and trailers. In addition to these items of storage, two other categories are at risk: washing hung out to dry and various garden ornaments (pots, gates, hanging baskets and small conifers).

Thefts from washing lines
Perhaps surprisingly, there appears to be some attraction in stealing clothes from washing lines. Repeated reports of this kind of theft were recognized in the first study when it was found to be much more common in Northampton than in Harrow. In fact at 33 thefts per 10 000 households in Northampton it had to be regarded as a significant problem, as it was almost as common in that data as burglaries involving electrical goods. The figure is lower in the 1987 Northampton data (*Table 8.1*), suggesting that this type of theft may be more common in the older nineteenth-century housing near the centre of the town, which was excluded from our 1987 data.

We know little about the offenders because none of them was caught in the crimes recorded in the first study, although in two cases men had been seen attempting such thefts and had run off. Since some of the early cases we considered involved mainly women's underwear, it was suggested that there may be some sexual significance in the crime, but further cases suggested that the motivation was more likely to be 'straight' theft. All kinds of clothing are taken, belonging to both sexes, and also towels and linen were frequently stolen. In two reports, other items were stolen at the same time including milk and a sports bag. In one incident the washing line was cut, presumably to make the theft easier and quicker.

The crime seems essentially opportunist in the correct sense of the word. On visiting houses where thefts had occurred in

Northampton, we found that most of the washing lines could be easily seen from well-used paths or alleyways. It seemed likely that the items stolen had caught the eye of the thief as he passed, even at night. In most cases access could be gained through a back gate, but in one or two cases the offender had probably climbed a wall or fence. The pattern in Harrow was different. There was very little of this kind of theft reported. Most likely, this is explained by the different environment. In Harrow most back gardens are out of sight from any public access, backing onto other gardens with no public pathway at the side of houses. In this way there would be little chance of washing attracting criminal attention.

Bicycles

The problem of bicycle thefts from garages was discussed in the previous chapter, but they are also stolen from the front and back gardens of houses. Although it is possible to separate the problem of front and back gardens, we believe that there is good reason to consider the problem as a whole.

In residential areas the main victims of bicycle theft appear to be children. Out of 49 incidents of cycle theft in the first study 30 of the victims were schoolboys. In much the same way as we believe bicycles are often removed from garages when they are left unlocked with the doors open, we imagine that most cycle thefts arise because children leave bicycles unattended in front gardens or driveways, or in back gardens where back gates are left open onto communal pathways or parking courts. The difference in the pattern of theft in Northampton and Harrow supports this hypothesis.

The data in *Table 8.3* are based on only a small sample of thefts, but they show that bicycles are more likely to be taken from the front gardens in Harrow and from back gardens in

TABLE 8.3 Location of bicycle thefts in Harrow and Northampton, 1982

	Harrow	*Northampton*	
	1982	*1982*	*1987*
Front garden or driveway	12	3	14
Back garden	5	11	19
Not known, elsewhere	9	9	26

(Source: Poyner, Helson and Webb, 1985)

Northampton. This difference seems to be caused by the predominant difference in housing in the two locations. In Harrow, as we have already noted, the back gardens are generally out of sight of public areas. Many houses are semi-detached with gardens planned back-to-back and side-by-side in the conventional manner and with few back alleyways. In Northampton, there is much terraced housing with rear gardens only accessible through back gates off communal paths and parking courts. It is easy to imagine with children playing in this kind of housing that these back gates are frequently left open. Furthermore their slatted construction in much of Northampton's new housing makes it easy to see into the garden and to reach any bolt fitted on the inside (see *Figure 8.3*).

Another reason for Harrow to have more theft from the front garden is that in many streets the access at the side of the house to the back garden is blocked by the later construction of a garage or shed (*Figure 8.4*). Because of the narrowness of this side access there was often barely enough space for the garage. The effect of this would be to make acces from the front to the back garden more difficult, because access to the back would be through two sets of garage or shed doors, and so it is easy to imagine that this would increase the probability of bicycles being left unattended at the front.

All these scenarios for cycle theft suggest much the same remedy. Bicycles will be used particularly by children and they will be left wherever convenient outside the house. The safest place must be in some secure area such as a properly fenced or walled back yard and, to make sure that such a yard is used, the access gate must be easy to use and well supervised from inside the house.

Figure 8.4 Housing in Harrow with side access filled in by garages.

Motorcycles

Motorcycles and mopeds formed a comparatively small group of residential crimes in the 1982 data in *Table 2.1*, but in the 1987 data for Northampton they formed a substantial element, amounting to nearly one theft for every 100 households. It would appear that motorcycles are stolen when they are left in vulnerable places. From both observation of housing estates and by examining the crime data it appears that owners do not have the opportunity to store motorcycles in secure places. In terraced housing with no rear access of adequate width, the only place to leave a motorcycle is on the front garden or in the street. The use of a garage would probably help to provide a secure storage place, but for the most part terraced housing often has limited garaging or none at all.

Sheds

Thefts from sheds are similar to those from garages in that they involve a variety of tools, particularly power tools and lawnmowers. Some bicycles were also stolen, often along with other tools. Our problem with taking the analysis further is that in the more recent data we were not given the exact addresses of these crimes and so could not contemplate a detailed analysis of the characteristics of the sheds, such as their location in relation to the house and so cannot make recommendations. However, bearing in mind the findings on garages, it seems likely that sheds close to the house and easily supervised from the house would be safer than those some distance away. Similarly, sheds in well-fenced or walled yards are likely to be more secure than elsewhere.

Implications for layout

Together these problems of security outside the house do point to a need for a secure area outside the house but adjacent to it and well supervised from it. A back garden is commonly provided in much modern housing. The well-known Essex County Council guide (1983: 34) states as policy that:

'*New houses shall have an outdoor sitting area not overlooked by adjacent or opposing outdoor sitting areas or living rooms; this requirement to be achieved by the design and layout of above eye-level* permanent *structures and walls.*'

This requirement is aimed at privacy and amenity, but it is clear that it could be easily extended to include security. The 'private zone' should be enclosed completely to make access only possible by climbing over a fence or wall or entering by a well-guarded gate.

The main problem of providing a satisfactory secure back yard or garden to houses is not so much the need for walls and fences but the provision of the secure gate access. As soon as some form of terraced design is contemplated, there is the obvious temptation to provide a back gate opening off a footpath at the back of the house. The data presented here and in previous chapters suggests that this is a vulnerable design in terms of crime. Rear access also makes the garden or yard less functional as a secure storage place for items such as bicycles and motorcycles because it is inconvenient and often physically difficult to take them around the back.

The most secure form of back garden or yard is where gardens are planned back-to-back and side-by-side. This is certainly the characteristic form of the low-crime areas in *Figure 8.1* such as 10, 11, 12, 13 and 14. The question then arises as to how best to provide access to the rear garden from the front. The most 'defensible' location for a gate at the front of the house must be close to the front door or windows where it is most likely that in and out movements can be supervised from inside the house. The detached and semi-detached house forms have a lot of advantages for the designer as they provide ready opportunities for direct access from the front to the back. *Figure 8.5* shows the arrangement not uncommon during the 1930s of a semi-detached house with garage. A valuable additional feature of these designs is the use of side windows to increase the surveillance of the side access. What is also important is that the access is not too narrow so that larger items of equipment as well as motorcycles can easily be taken through. A minimum of a

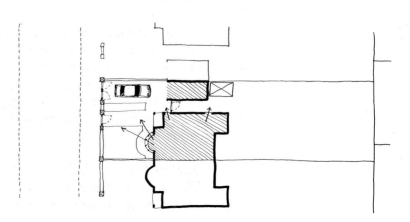

Figure 8.5 Typical 1930s semi-detached housing showing controlled access to the back garden from the front.

metre width might help to encourage its use. A further improvement for access to the secure yard in some modern housing designs is to provide full-width doors at both ends of the garage, which allows some equipment like boats and trailers to be stored securely in the back yard rather than left at the front of the house.

The front of the house

Having dealt with rear garden thefts and bicycles and motorcycles, there is a somewhat smaller group of thefts from the front of houses. Most of these thefts relate to the area around the front door and include the theft of milk bottles and items left at the doorstep by various delivery services. In our more recent 1987 data we noticed a new category of items taken from meter cupboards which seems to show that there is a need to have somewhere secure and under cover to leave deliveries. These cupboards are often provided in more recently built housing to give access to electricity and gas meters.

The theft of milk bottles from doorsteps is referred to by Farrington and Dowds (1985) as a very common type of crime frequently mentioned in crime surveys but erratically reported by the police. This may partly explain why no such crimes appeared in the Metropolitan Police records for Harrow, but they were reported in both our Northampton samples. In the more recent Northampton 1987 data, milk bottles were not the most common items. There were also items such as bread and other food stuffs, now commonly delivered by milk roundsmen, along with parcels. This may well illustrate the newer trends in the development of marketing delivery services and in the increase of mail-order retailing.

The numbers of recorded incidents are small but when we visited the locations of some of these crimes during the first study we found that the situations from which milk was stolen were all similar. Most often it was from older terraced houses with doors which open directly on to the street or from new-town terraced housing where footpaths ran close to the front doors of houses and where there were no houses facing.

Implications for design
The issue of deliveries and servicing to houses does seem important in relation to security problems. It is difficult to

establish from the small number of crimes what precise conditions would help to reduce these thefts. For example, it might be argued that having low walls around the front garden would reduce access and theft but there are plenty of housing areas without front walls which have no sign of this problem. The most important factor seems to be the short open fronts of terraced houses where the paths run close to the front of houses and the lack of surveillance from other houses opposite. Once the path is located further away from the front door few thefts occur.

In good design it seems that there must be a case for providing access to meters and rubbish bins, etc., at the front of the house for the various services, without the need to gain access to the secure yard. It should be comparatively easy to provide somewhere to leave deliveries out of sight of passers-by. Perhaps this is one of the reasons why the enclosed porch additions are so popular in the improvement of housing, particularly terraced council housing once sold into private ownership (*Figure 8.6*). The provision for rubbish bins, the reading of meters and the leaving of deliveries should be given more thought by housing designers.

Figure 8.6 One reason for the popularity of adding porches to houses, particularly on privatized council estates, may be to provide a safe place for deliveries of milk, bread, mail orders, etc.

Theft of garden items
One final group of thefts around the house is the taking of ornamental items, particularly from the front garden. The range of items reported as stolen included concrete urns, ornamental trees such as dwarf conifers, gates, parts of fences, hanging baskets, ornamental seats and a concrete frog.

In the earlier study we concluded that these thefts had some affinity with vandalism in that some of the thefts seem to be more like pranks or skylarking and probably involve a little drunkenness in some cases. The thefts usually occurred overnight. It was noticeable that the houses selected as targets tended to be somewhat differentiated from neighbouring houses. Up-market houses, in particular, received this kind of attention, as well as houses that had well-kept fronts or large amounts of ornamentation at the front (see the house in the foreground in *Figure 1.3(a)*).

Although this type of theft is a nuisance to the households that suffer the loss, it is difficult to imagine any generally useful design guidance. It is true to say that most of the thefts were from open-fronted gardens, but then the number of incidents was too small to claim that fenced or walled front gardens would be less at risk.

In the first study we thought that there was some pattern of distribution in Harrow: 'All the incidents occur in pedestrian routes used by groups of youths returning home at night. The routes are from pubs, tube stations, general centres of evening life.' The conclusion suggested was that 'design of garden spaces in front of houses should be more carefully related to the use of the roadway or footpath immediately beyond it. In a little-used area the problem will not arise, but if the path or roadway is likely to be used as a main pedestrian through-route, then the use of walls and protective planting may be appropriate'. (*Figure 8.7.*)

Perhaps the most reliable action could be taken by residents themselves who could do more to select forms of garden ornamentation which are less easily stolen. Large concrete planters or well-established shrubs are unlikely to be carried off as a joke by inebriated youths.

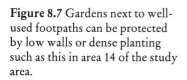

Figure 8.7 Gardens next to well-used footpaths can be protected by low walls or dense planting such as this in area 14 of the study area.

9 Criminal damage

Vandalism has always been associated with housing and crime, and in the UK, particularly with council housing. It is interesting that the first major UK research on Oscar Newman's 'defensible space' theory was a study of vandalism on council estates in London (Wilson, 1980). More recently the work of Alice Coleman was first published as a study of the relationship between design and nuisance behaviour (damage, litter, graffiti, faeces and urine) rather than crime (Coleman, 1985).

In England and Wales, the police term for vandalism is 'criminal damage' which is restricted to damage which costs more than £20 to put right. The advantage of this definition is that it ensures that some appreciable damage is done before it is categorized as a crime, but it also means that a good deal of genuine nuisance behaviour which is reported to the police will not be recorded as crime. It must also depend on how damage is repaired. A small pane of broken glass in a private house repaired by the home owner with well-developed DIY skills may cost little in money terms but if the same owner were to call in a local builder to do the work, the cost would be more substantial. Indeed, when we look at the incidents reported as criminal damage, broken windows are the most common items.

A further problem in deciding the nature of criminal damage is that it is difficult to establish the motive behind the damage. An incident of damage such as a broken window may be the result of unintentional or accidental behaviour such as a ball game or it could be intentional. If intentional it may have been caused by young people larking about, done out of spite or as a result of some argument or dispute. Equally possible, it may have been an attempted burglary which went wrong because the burglar was disturbed or because he injured himself on the glass and gave up his attempt. There is evidence from detailed reading of police reports that all these interpretations are possible and justified in different cases, but because evidence was inadequate the police recorded 'criminal damage' to be on the safe side.

In the first study our data were the original police reports and from reading these we were convinced that many of the broken windows reported in the Harrow data could be

TABLE 9.1 Criminal damage to residential property in Harrow and Northampton, 1982 (rate per 10 000 households)

	Harrow	*Northampton*
Rowdy youths	13	5
Victimization		
(a) Asians	22	–
(b) Other	10	14
Air gun attacks	4	–
Arson	1	9
Other	3	3
	53	31

(Source: Poyner, Helson and Webb, 1985)

described as victimization of the Asian community, because a disproportionate number of complaints came from individuals with Asian names. But such interpretations are always open to the objection that such a community may feel more victimized and therefore interpret every item of damage as victimization, even if it was accidental. The figures produced from that analysis are shown in *Table 9.1.*

Those who may be doubtful about the likelihood of Asian victimization should appreciate that according to the 1981 census the population in our study area of Harrow with the head of household being born in the New Commonwealth or Pakistan averaged 16.14%, rising to 27% in one of the wards. By comparison in Northampton this group of the population constituted only 4.82%.

Broken windows were by far the most common type of damage and the victims lived on or near council housing estates. Many of the households reported several attacks in the same year (37 attacks on 22 households) and one household reported seven incidents in one year. The local authority was considering re-housing this family elsewhere.

The figures on criminal damage for the second study of Northampton 1987 data are not directly comparable with those for the earlier study. In this data we did not have access to police files or to precise addresses and so our understanding of the motives behind the damage was limited. We also had no information about victims. The result is a rather different classification given in *Table 9.2.* Almost certainly

TABLE 9.2 Criminal damage in residential areas of north-east Northampton, 1987

Type of damage	N	Rate per 10 000 households
Stones and other objects through windows	68	49
Windows broken by airgun pellets	6	4
Other smashed windows	23	16
Door glass broken	16	11
Doors/windows forced	11	8
Garden fences, walls, and gates damaged	24	17
Following an argument	16	11
Internal damage to houses and garages	9	8
Other damage to outside of houses	11	6
Other damage not to house or garage	10	7
	194	137

some of these cases would be reallocated to 'attempted burglary' if more details had been available. Damage to garage doors has been dealt with in Chapter 7.

The incidents which are recorded as the result of some argument seem to arise from personal relationships which have broken down. The offenders are often referred to as ex-boyfriends or ex-husbands of the victims, and it seems clear that this category is another version of domestic violence. It seems likely that this is also the reason behind damage to the inside of houses.

Implications for design and layout

It is possible that some forms of victimization would be related to the position or location of houses, in that a prominent location might attract attention or that a house might be more exposed to a public footpath, etc., but we do not feel that there is sufficient evidence to make any proposals which relate to design or layout. Similarly for internal damage to property or where the damage is the result of a personal dispute, it seems unlikely that design or layout would have much influence on such behaviour.

Perhaps more promising is the question of damage caused by rowdy youths (as defined in the first study). These are incidents where house windows or garden walls and fences are deliberately broken or damaged for no apparent reason

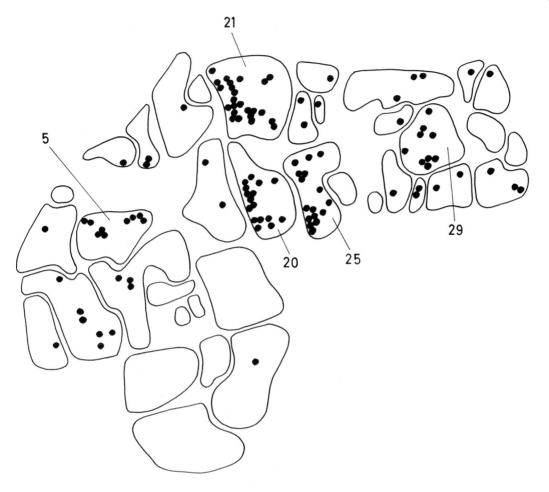

Figure 9.1 The distribution of criminal damage involving broken glass in doors or windows in north-east Northampton, 1987.

and where rowdy youths are believed to be the offenders. Damage seems to have been caused by throwing stones at windows and kicking at walls and fences. Some attempt was made to plot the locations of damage to fences, walls and gates and to see if this might be related to the theft of garden ornamental items referred to in the previous chapter, but the number of incidents was too small to reveal any pattern.

Leaving these categories aside, the main bulk of criminal damage involves windows and doors – particularly the breakage of glass. In an effort to find some useful pattern which might relate to design and layout, the first five categories in *Table 9.2* were plotted on the map of housing areas. The result is given in *Figure 9.1*.

This distribution is by no means random. More than 80% of the reported damage is in public sector housing. Where it does occur in the private housing areas there are only one or two isolated incidents. Even within the public sector there is a

Figure 9.2 Housing where significant numbers of broken windows are reported are in the public sector with pedestrian-only communal greens close to the front of houses. This view is taken in area 5.

clear concentration on areas patches 20, 21 and 25 with 29 and 5 showing less of a problem. All these areas are large public housing estates and unlike other housing areas the houses face onto communal greens with footpaths often running close to the front of the houses. At the same time the small front gardens are usually open grass areas (*Figure 9.2*). It is easy to imagine that such design forms do promote the more rowdy activities of youths and children which lead to damage of the type described. If this design form does create the increased risk, then the remedy would be to avoid designs with communal greens in front of housing. Although the thinness of our data would lead us to be cautious about making a strong recommendation, it has to be admitted that housing layouts with conventional streets had little trouble.

One further thought that does occur with this map distribution is that the reporting of damage may be influenced by the housing tenure. In the case of the private sector the responsibility for repair is always on the householder. It is true that serious damage may well involve an insurance claim, but unlike burglary or autocrime, insurance companies would probably not be too much concerned about the damage being of a criminal or accidental nature or even caused by natural phenomena (storms and birds, etc.). It occurs to us that on the local authority estate, the damage would be repaired by the authority, and the reporting of an incident to the police may be seen as one way to establish that the tenant was not at fault and that he or she was in some way a victim. Such an interpretation of damage would go some way to explaining the predominance of vandalism as a public sector housing issue. Is it possible that one way to reduce reported damage, and therefore the crime statistics, is to privatize tenure or redefine tenants' responsibilities?

10 Explaining the patterns of crime

This study was based on an analysis of 38 housing areas, each of which had a different layout design and a resulting different crime profile. To explain the pattern of crime in terms of our findings in all these areas would take too much space, but we do think that it is interesting to illustrate, for some of these areas, how different layout designs affect crime. To do this we have selected eight areas for detailed consideration.

Area 25: A high-crime area

There were several areas of particularly high crime levels which could be chosen. All of them are public sector housing built during the 1970s as part of the new town expansion of Northampton. *Figure 10.1* is taken from a map of a small area within area 25 which, more than any other area, illustrates the

Figure 10.1 Part of area 25. (Source: Ordnance Survey (adapted).)

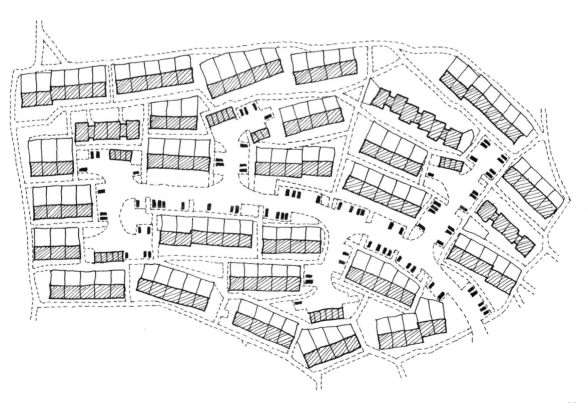

bad features of design which create crime problems. The houses are mostly laid out with backs facing fronts rather than face-to-face. There are pathways to give access to gates at the back of all rear gardens, and cars are parked in large communal areas. There are small groups of garages associated with these parking areas, but none is linked directly to any houses. The pathway system amounts to a complex through network so that most paths run closely across the fronts of houses and along the backs, and each path leads off quickly in many directions with many intersections with other paths.

It is easy to see how accessible the back gardens are and how little protection the fronts of these houses have, and how easy it would be for potential criminals to explore the area at will and disappear on foot in a matter of seconds.

The result of this design is that we find that area 25 had a high rate for nearly all crimes: theft of cars, both kinds of burglary, theft from outside the house, and problems of criminal damage. Compared to some other areas it is slightly less of a problem for theft from cars, but the area is still troubled by this crime. The overall crime rate is calculated at 22.4 per 100 households. It is clear from all the data presented in the previous chapters that the design of this area is a disaster from the crime prevention point of view.

Low-crime areas

Both areas 12 (*Figure 10.2*) and 15 are generally low-crime areas, and are interesting to look at because one is a public sector area and the other is a private sector development. Both were built in the late 1960s.

Area 12 is built around a spine road with a series of smaller culs-de-sac and loops attached. The houses are mainly detached, but there are some semi-detached and short terraces. All have open fronts with their own driveway and garage, and there is usually access from the front to a fenced garden behind through a full-height side gate. The houses have large single-pane windows facing the street. These houses were built before the more recent concern for energy conservation in housing design, and so wherever you walk on the streets there are always large glass windows in front of you. The way houses on corners are angled so that they face you all the time is particularly striking, even intimidating (*Figure 10.3*). Many of the culs-de-sac in this area are on a gradient so that the houses in these lie above the main spine road. Just one window in the house at the end of the

Figure 10.2 Part of area 12. (Source: Ordnance Survey (adapted).)

cul-de-sac, directly opposite the entrance off the spine road, can dominate the approach to the cul-de-sac. All this contributes to a very powerful impression of continual natural surveillance. Although the houses are now matured, the front gardens have not been over-planted, and perhaps more than any other, this area of housing demonstrates the power of mutual surveillance by neighbours.

The result of all this is very little crime on any of the maps produced in this study. The area has a low crime rate in all categories. The overall rate of crime in the study was 4.5 per

Figure 10.3 In area 12 there are always many large windows facing the street, and even the houses on corners are arranged to provide relentless 'watching' over the area.

100 households. If there are weaknesses in this layout it is that there is some footpath access to the open ground on the south side which according to our theories would encourage cash and jewelley burglary. Indeed, the elimination of these footpaths and the avoidance of the use of a through spine road may well have reduced the crime in this area to virtually zero.

The other low crime area is area 15 (*Figure 10.4*). The total crime rate was only slightly higher at 4.8 per 100 households, but it is particularly interesting to find terraced public sector housing with such a low crime rate. Early in our analysis of the 1987 data we were surprised that this area did not have more vehicle crime because there was much street parking and there were garage courts behind the terraces. Closer examination of the area showed that it was a very different environment from the high-crime areas such as 20, 21 and 25. Unlike those public-sector developments this area had a very much higher garage provision. Most houses have garages attached at the back, opening on to the garage courts. The design of these courts is such that only a limited number of cars can be left parked (otherwise they obstruct garages) and furthermore the courts are not pedestrian throughways. The net result of this design is to limit the number of cars at risk and to limit vehicle crime to a moderate level.

All other categories of crime were low. The strength of this layout seems to be in its surveillance characteristics. In most cases the paths and the street access are treated like conventional streets, with houses facing each other, and it does seem to support the idea that this particular design

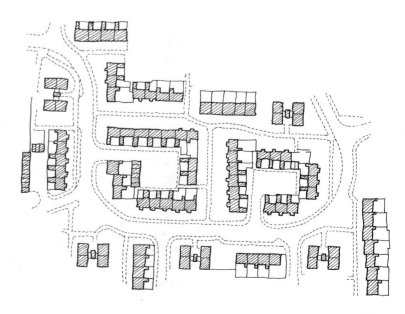

Figure 10.4 Part of area 15. (Source: Ordnance Survey (adapted).)

Figure 10.5 The strength of the layout of area 15 seems to be in its surveillance characteristics. For example, houses are so planned around road junctions that they supervise the through spine road intensively.

Figure 10.6 The garage courts in area 15 are surrounded by houses whose rear first-floor windows look out over the court and its entrance.

characteristic is probably more important to crime prevention than any other. Like area 12, surveillance is good on corners so that the roads are constantly overlooked by houses (*Figure 10.5*). The garage courts are surrounded by houses whose rear first-floor windows look out over the court and its entrance (*Figure 10.6*).

Another public sector housing area in the study which gave rise to considerable interest was area 31 (see *Figure 5.6*). For most categories of crime there was almost no sign of criminal behaviour. The one exception was theft from cars which was a notable problem. We found it difficult to explain why these houses with hardstanding for cars at the front had no theft of cars, but quite a lot of theft from cars (*Figure 10.7*).

The reason for this curious problem became clear when we discovered the relationship between pedestrian-only pathways passing through housing areas and thefts from cars.

Area 31 is riddled with such footways which pass along its boundary, cut through the groups of houses, and connect the area to neighbouring housing areas. Clearly, potential thieves regard it as far too risky to try to steal a car because that means starting it up and driving it out of a cul-de-sac which is heavily supervised by the surrounding houses. The presence of paths, however, makes stealing things from cars relatively simple, as thieves can easily slip away to the neighbouring path network.

When we originally visited the area we thought that the footways did not give access to the rear gardens of these terraced houses, like area 25, and that this explained the low level of burglary in the area. It was not until our third or fourth visit to this group of houses that we discovered that some of these footways did in fact cut through the housing and pass along the bottom of rear gardens which had low fences and gates. How was it, then, that this area only suffered low levels of burglary? The reason seems to be that, although this area appears to share the same very vulnerable design feature as that which gives so much trouble in areas such as 25, the environments are in reality very different.

The paths running around an area like 25 are clearly very public footways over which surveillance is difficult and control non-existent (see *Figure 10.1*). They are single-loaded pathways, flanked on one side by high rear garden fences (see *Figure 8.2*). On the other side they are often flanked by fronts of terraces. These pathways are also often flanked on one side not by houses but by open ground, communal car parking areas, and even blank high brick walls. The housing is planned in short rows back to front so that the ends of terraces are not overlooked directly at all, and often have patches of rough grass and pathway junctions next to them.

In contrast the pathways passing along the backs of the housing in area 31 have been designed as much more private areas which are controlled and supervised by house occupants. The housing is separated into small groups of houses which are arranged back-to-back to form a protective 'courtyard' type of area in the centre through which the pathways pass (see *Figure 5.6*). Access into these back paths is only through narrow alleyways which are not easily noticed on first driving into the area. The rear gardens of houses at the ends of terraces at these access points are protected with high walls. Children's play areas are provided in these central areas, and the effect of all this is that these areas become an extension of the rear gardens (*Figure 10.8*). There is good

Figure 10.7 Cars parked on hard-standing in front of houses in area 31 are not stolen but are often broken into.

Figure 10.8 Houses in area 31 are designed so that these play areas are an extension of rear gardens, and occupants exercise considerable control over these areas through which the pathways pass.

supervision from the surrounding houses, as gardens only have small waist-high fences, and parents can and do easily control their children in these play areas. In effect, the houses in area 31 have been designed 'inside out' so that the rear gardens become the front gardens which face onto a well-supervised pedestrian cul-de-sac.

Two areas with moderate crime problems

Area 6, with crime rate of 7.2 per 100 households, is an example of 1930s private development much admired by Professor Coleman (see *Figure 3.7*). It does in fact have some low crime rates in two categories, on theft of cars and electrical goods burglary. The reason for the low number of thefts of cars is that most houses have driveways and a garage, and the reason for the comparatively low burglary rates is that access to the rear is not easy and there are few opportunities for escape from these long and well-supervised streets (*Figure 10.9*). What seems to make this kind of development just a little more vulnerable than an area such as area 12 is that the houses are arranged on streets, all of which are pedestrian through-routes. This through movement of people does seem to encourage medium rates of crime for theft from cars, of cash and jewellery, and from outside the house.

Area 33 has a more specific problem (*Figure 10.10*). The overall crime rate of 9.3 per 100 households is due mainly to the burglary of electrical goods. It was discovered that it is

Figure 10.9 Part of area 6. (Source: Ordnance Survey (adapted).)

Figure 10.10 Part of area 33. (Source: Ordnance Survey (adapted).)

comparatively easy to get to the back of many of the houses in this area. The houses have driveways, and therefore there is little theft of cars, but the builder only left spaces for garages to be built, and in many houses the owners have not yet constructed their own garage, leaving the side access to the back garden wide open (see *Figure 10.11*). The other weakness of this layout is that two pedestrian routes run through the area separate from the road system, but connected to the ends of culs-de-sac by footpaths. We feel that access to back gardens and the presence of an extensive footpath system has made this area of housing more vulnerable than need be.

Figure 10.11 It is comparatively easy to get access to the rear of houses in area 33.

Two more up-market areas with crime problems

Both these areas are made up of larger detached houses. Area 11 was built in the late 1920s and has an overall crime rate of 12.2 per 100 households, and area 14, built quite recently, has an overall rate of 12.5 per 100 households. Both areas can be described as up-market housing.

The frontages to area 11 (*Figure 10.12*) are conventional modest gardens with front walls and sometimes the original gates still exist. There is quite a lot of established foliage and trees both in the front and the back gardens. The only crime category that is low for this area is the theft of cars, and it is quite clear that this is because most houses have their own driveways and garages. However, the streets in this area are all useful walk-through routes linking with a path across a neighbouring park which leads to the town centre. It may be that this attracts quite a lot of pedestrian movement which helps to encourage potential criminals, and this coupled with the relatively easy access to the backs of these houses and the ample cover given by mature planting means that there is a moderate amount of crime in most categories. It was particularly attractive to burglars interested in cash and jewellery, and this is easily understood in terms of these environmental factors and the fact that some of these houses are likely to be occupied by more wealthy people. The road system also makes escape comparatively easy (*Figure 10.13*).

Area 14 is physically very different from all other areas of housing in that it consists of large modern detached houses (*Figure 10.14*) off a series of quiet loop roads (*Figure 10.15*). The low density makes access round the houses comparatively easy, and the fact that a pathway system runs through the area (*Figure 10.16*) seems to contribute to the two crime problems which are theft from cars and cash and jewellery burglary. Areas of graffiti and the use of barbed wire by householders on fencing adjacent to the pathways is also evidence that the pathway system is a problem. It is clear that such an area would attract prospective thieves, and apparently it does, despite the large number of alarms fitted to the houses.

Figure 10.12 Tree-lined established roads in area 11.

Figure 10.13 Part of area 11. (Source: Ordnance Survey (adapted).)

Figure 10.14 Newer up-market housing in area 14.

Figure 10.16 The pathway system running through this area is a vulnerable design feature, and contributes to the two crime problems of cash and jewellery burglary and theft from cars.

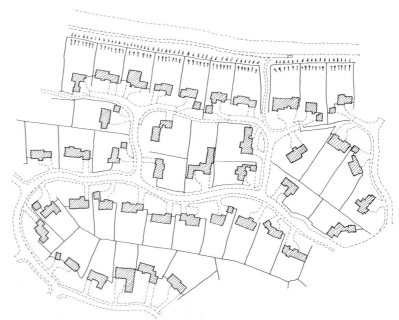

Figure 10.15 Part of area 14 with up-market housing. (Source: Ordnance Survey (adapted).)

11 Requirements for crime free housing

In this chapter we try to draw together our findings in a form which designers can easily use as a checklist. We summarize each of the findings in the order they have appeared in the book so far, explaining their relation to crime control. In the second part of the chapter we identify 12 requirements which we consider to be the main elements that are necessary in the design and layout of housing to achieve a crime free environment.

Theft of cars (Chapter 5)

The main finding is that each house should have a driveway or hardstanding in front of the house for the parking of a car. Garages may also be desirable, and they have other advantages in that they provide additional storage, but they do not seem to be an essential ingredient for preventing theft of cars. Essentially, what should be avoided is parking in the street or communal parking areas away from the house, and particularly if they are out of sight at the back or at the side of housing.

Theft from cars (Chapter 5)

The provision of a driveway or hardstanding in front of the house also relates to preventing theft from cars, but we find that this form of theft is far more extensive and occurs in many more locations than theft of cars. It seems that to control this more virulent form of crime we also need to avoid through pedestrian routes within individual housing blocks or areas. It would be better for pathway access into housing areas to be branch-like, following the road system rather than creating many through-routes and additional pathways in and out of the housing area.

Burglary of electrical goods (Chapter 6)

The burglary of electrical goods appears to rely on the use of the car, and so an environment which inhibits burglars leaving cars in and around housing should discourage burglary.

Roadways into housing areas should be as heavily supervised as possible by the houses they serve. Houses should face on to the roadway with as many windows as possible. A useful characteristic of layout would be for houses to be clustered around entry points so that a large number of houses face onto a small stretch of roadway immediately at the entrance to a housing area.

Since the most vulnerable approach to the house must be the front of the house where it is intended for visitors and strangers, etc., to arrive, it is important that the layout takes full advantage of the potential surveillance by neighbours of anyone coming and going to the house. If houses are planned facing each other across the street we find less risk of burglary. If houses are grouped together along the street they will be even more effective at providing mutual surveillance.

Access to the back of a house should be restricted by enclosing the back garden or yard by a full-height wall or fence. Back alleyways and gates should be avoided, and the most satisfactory arrangement is where gardens are planned side-by-side and back-to-back.

Avoid creating pedestrian routes through housing areas, as this encourages search behaviour by potential thieves. It gives them the opportunity to wander freely through any housing area without looking out of place.

Similarly to the above, it seems to be important to avoid creating pedestrian escape routes out of housing areas. It is common practice in modern housing design to provide short cuts at the ends of culs-de-sac or at corners in road systems. It seems preferable always to combine pedestrian routes and car routes so that offenders cannot escape without potentially being followed by a car.

Burglary of cash and jewellery (Chapter 6)

This kind of burglary is normally carried out on foot, which makes the offender more mobile and less concerned about access by car. Offenders need to search for suitable targets, and it seems that reducing access points to a housing area reduces the risk of this kind of burglary, presumably because it reduces the opportunity for casual search by potential criminals.

It may reduce the risk of this kind of burglary to limit the cover from planting, particularly large evergreen shrubs at the front of the house. It should be noted that this kind of burglary did not seem to be influenced by surveillance from houses across the street. It seems more important to the offender that there is cover close to the house itself. Further evidence for this is that deep back gardens with mature planting also appear to benefit this kind of burglary. As with electrical goods burglary, it is important to reduce access to the back of the house.

Theft from garages (Chapter 7)

Although garages are not essential for protecting cars, they do offer some secure storage for bicycles, motorcycles, tools and garden equipment, including lawnmowers, and are therefore valuable in reducing theft. However, it is important that garages are located close to the house, preferably with the front doors facing the street and near the front of the house. There is clear evidence that once so located only minimal security is required to secure the garage.

It is probably important to place the garage doors at least a car length from the public roadway or footpath to discourage theft when doors are left open even for short periods.

Theft from around the house (Chapter 8)

It is important to provide a secure yard at the side or rear of the house which can only be entered from the front under supervision from the house. Access should be via a gate at the front which can be locked on the inside. The access should not be too narrow, say at least one metre. The purpose of this is to provide a safe place to hang out washing and keep garden equipment, recreational furniture, bicycles and tools or even motorcycles. It is also an area in which storage sheds and the like should be located.

Mutual surveillance by houses opposite is also important for controlling this kind of theft as has already been mentioned under electrical goods burglary. Increasing the risk of a neighbour seeing a theft take place must deter potential thieves from taking things from front gardens and doorsteps or from gaining illicit entry to the secure yard or back garden.

It is helpful to have the front door at some distance from the public street or path. This, no doubt increases control over access to the front door and side access through surveillance from the house and by neighbours. It might have been expected that low front walls around the front garden would increase this effect, but the data from the study did not support this.

There is a need for somewhere close to the front door to leave deliveries out of sight from the street, such as in a porch or behind a low enclosing wall. It is also important that access to dustbins and gas and electricity meters should be possible without having to gain access to the secure area at the back or side of the house.

Criminal damage (Chapter 9)

Avoid planning houses facing onto green areas with only footpath access. It seems that this kind of setting is more likely to suffer from window breakage of criminal and probably non-criminal kinds. It would be better to locate green areas outside the housing areas.

These findings can be edited into specific requirements for design. There is a certain amount of overlapping in the above list of findings so that similar design requirements can emerge from different crime problems. What follows is a summary of the design requirements which we have found likely to produce crime free housing.

The house itself

First of all we have the idea of a house for an individual or family, or any small group living together. The notion implied by the word 'household' is that within this group there is sufficient trust and social control that material goods and property are either held in common or else there is a well-established system of recognizing and respecting individuals' property. The house provides a safe place to keep the property of this social group and a secure place to live.

Requirement 1 – Moderate locking security
The protection provided by the fabric of the house has to be sufficient to keep out the weather and deny unhindered access by potential thieves to household property. In general our Anglo-Saxon culture has arrived at a level of security which prevents ready access by locking doors and providing secure fixings to windows but does not unduly interfere with the daily activities of the occupants. Many recent guidelines on domestic security advocate keyed locking devices for

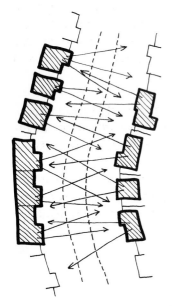

Figure 11.1 Houses should face each other across the street.

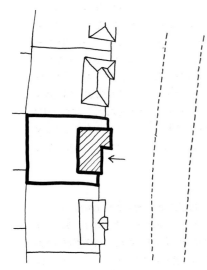

Figure 11.2 High fences to prevent access to the rear of a house.

windows and key-operated bolts as well as extra locks on doors, but the evidence is uncertain how far these additional locking devices reduce the risk of crime. Given the opportunity, a determined thief will always be able to overcome security devices. What this study suggests is that *houses require only a moderate level of locking security, provided the opportunity for crime is controlled by the design and layout of a housing area.* To rely only on security hardware may also lead us to the kind of fortress society already illustrated in the introduction to this book.

Requirement 2 – Facing windows

Where a number of houses are built together there is an opportunity for the mutual protection of a community. For self-evident economic reasons a group of houses will share the same communal access routes, in the forms of paths, roads, streets, carways, etc. In general this will mean that the entrance to an individual house will face communal access routes. *The front windows of houses should face each other across the street or similar shared access area, to create a system of mutual surveillance*, in which anyone coming and going to a house may be seen by neighbours. The fronts of houses should not be obscured by fences, walls, or substantial foliage which can provide hiding places. Mutual surveillance can be built into the housing without any need for special organization or the setting up of any formal collaboration by neighbours (*Figure 11.1*).

Requirement 3 – High fences at the sides and rear

Although the front of the house can be protected by surveillance from neighbours, it is unlikely that similar levels of mutual surveillance can be achieved for the other sides of the house. To prevent easy access to doors or windows at the sides and rear of the house *the side and rear boundaries of individual house plots should be provided with full-height fencing or walls.* This provision will only be effective if plot sizes are moderately small, allowing some surveillance of the boundaries from inside the house. The fencing of boundaries will be even more effective where they back onto other private garden areas, as this further reduces the opportunity for thieves to gain access and may allow some mutual surveillance of boundaries by neighbours (*Figure 11.2*).

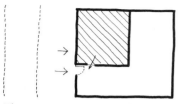

Figure 11.3 A secure yard or garden at the side or back of the house accessible at the front.

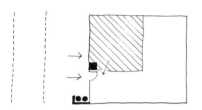

Figure 11.4 Provision for waste bins, meters, and somewhere to leave deliveries under cover and out of sight, should be made at the front of the house.

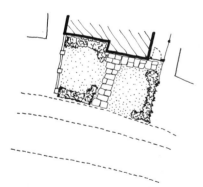

Figure 11.5 A private space between the public path and the front door to a house.

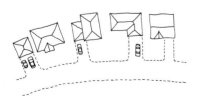

Figure 11.6 Driveways or hardstandings in front of houses.

Requirement 4 – Front access to a secure yard

Requirement 3 may create a secure yard or garden but an important additional requirement is that *there should be a gateway at the front of the house giving access to a secure yard or garden area. This gateway should be designed so that it can be locked or bolted on the inside and supervised from inside the house.* The gateway should be wide enough for garden equipment and motorcycles, etc. (about a metre). The purpose of the yard is to provide a secure place to dry washing, leave bicycles, motorcycles, garden furniture and other equipment (*Figure 11.3*).

Requirement 5 – Access for servicing and deliveries

There should be a place to store waste bins and provide access to gas and electricity meters at the front of the house to avoid the need to enter the secure yard. *It is also desirable to provide a place by the front door where deliveries can be left under cover and out of sight of the public footpath* to protect items such as milk, groceries and parcels from theft (*Figure 11.4*).

Requirement 6 – Space at the front

There seems to be a need for an area in front of the house between the house and public access areas (paths or roadways). The popular demand for a front garden may be more to do with privacy than security, but it seems to function in a number of ways to increase security both for burglary and theft of items left on doorsteps, etc. A minimum distance would be around 3 metres, but more would be desirable. The evidence is weak but the introduction of low walls or planting around this front area may increase security to some extent, provided this does not lead to extensive bushy growth or other obstructions to surveillance from across the street (*Figure 11.5*).

Requirement 7 – On-curtilage hardstanding for cars

To control autocrime, *all car parking should be on hardstandings within the curtilage of the house, preferably at the front to facilitate surveillance* (*Figure 11.6*).

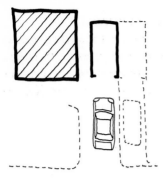

Requirement 8 – A garage at the side of the house

It is an advantage to provide a garage with each house, not only for even safer storage of vehicles but also for other equipment, tools, garden furniture, etc. *Any garage should be provided at the side of the house, close to the front entrance.* Note that a projecting garage can interfere with the mutual surveillance of houses opposite (*Figure 11.7*).

Figure 11.7 Garages next to the front of houses.

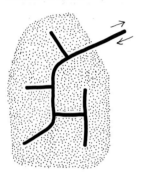

Housing areas

Requirement 9 – Limit road access

It is an advantage to reduce the number of road access points to an area of housing and to avoid creating through traffic routes. Such a pattern reduces the opportunity for potential criminals to search for potential targets, particularly in burglary (*Figure 11.8*).

Figure 11.8 Reduce access points to a housing area or neighbourhood.

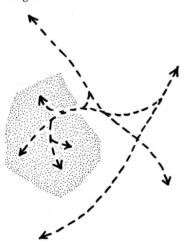

Requirement 10 – Avoid through pedestrian routes

Where pedestrian routes are separate from the roadways, they should not be planned to create a series of through routes connecting with other housing areas or open spaces. This not only reduces pedestrian access, and therefore search behaviour, but also reduces opportunities for easy escape. Ideally, pedestrian routes should follow car routes (*Figure 11.9*).

Figure 11.9 Pedestrian routes in a housing area should not be designed to provide through routes or escape routes.

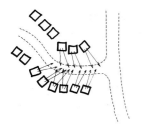

Figure 11.10 Road access overlooked by the houses it serves.

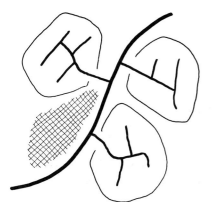

Figure 11.11 Green areas are best placed outside housing areas.

Requirement 11 – Surveillance of access roads

Houses should be oriented to face access routes and especially to focus on points of entry into an area to provide intensive surveillance. Such a pattern will discourage potential criminals from entering an area either on foot or by car (*Figure 11.10*).

Requirement 12 – Green spaces outside housing areas

Green open spaces should be provided near the entrances to housing areas rather than within them. Greens tend to attract youths and more rowdy activities which are best kept away from small groups of houses (*Figure 11.11*).

12 Implications for current practice

In this chapter we would like to review the implications oɩ our findings on the design guidance for the house-building industry. To do this we would like to tackle this question in two stages. The first is to compare our recommendations with other guidance on security in housing. Second, we look at a number of examples of current layout design to see how far the industry is already following these recommendations and to identify difficulties or objections which might arise.

Existing guidance on security in housing

At the time of writing we are not aware of guidance literature on housing layout and crime other than in the UK. We have seen and are aware of guides to building security in several countries which concentrate on locking systems, lighting and access control to buildings and groups of buildings, but we are not aware of guidance in the layout of housing estates or similar developments. The authors would be pleased to hear of any information about such guidance from any source in Europe and in any country around the world.

The focus of security measures has until very recently been on locking hardware and other supporting equipment such as lighting, access control, CCTV surveillance and various alarm systems. This 'security approach' has had a growing influence on crime prevention in residential settings and in the last year or so an increasing number of security alarms have been fitted to houses. It is reported that in the UK householders spent £175 million on household security in 1987 which was £35 million more than the previous year (*Crime Prevention News*, 1989(i)). Much of the literature produced by the crime prevention field focused on this 'security approach'. In many ways the first *British Standard Guide for: Security of buildings against crime* (British Standards Institution, 1986) epitomizes this view. It deals with the design and layout of housing estates in a very cursory manner and then goes on to two lengthy sections on window and door security.

The BSI document is cautious about the use of alarms and access control systems. Its main thrust is the improvement of locking standards by adding additional locks and hinge bolts or keyed bolts to doors and locks to opening windows. The emphasis on locking devices is further reflected in the short guide published by the Home Office in support of the British Standard (Home Office, 1986b).

The recommendations made in this book do not take the matter of security hardware quite so far as the BSI and Home Office. We tend to accept the findings of an earlier Home Office research study which suggested that 'although levels of security amongst households are generally low, burgled houses are distinguished from other houses not so much by the relative security protection but by surveillance and access opportunities' (Winchester and Jackson, 1982). This is certainly borne out by the research data presented in this book. It is almost certain that the most crime free housing areas of the study did not have any special additional locking features. The only area to have a noticeably larger number of alarm systems was the more well-to-do housing area labelled number 14 in the study maps. As we have concluded, most of our recommendations about layout relate to surveillance by neighbours and limiting access to houses and the neighbourhoods in which they are built.

Our earlier research report (Poyner, Helson and Webb, 1985) was completed by mid 1985 and presented at a seminar at the Tavistock Institute of Human Relations to an invited group of criminologists, housing architects and planners and police officers with an interest in the newly developing architectural liaison service. By that time the drafting of the BSI Guide, which had taken a number of years, was virtually complete and there was no likelihood of our research influencing its drafting. However, following a Prime Ministerial level initiative to encourage more active involvement of commerce and industry in crime prevention early in 1986, the National House-Building Council agreed to set up a working party under the chairmanship of Graham Pye to make recommendations about cost-effective security measures for new house building in the private sector.

The starting point for this working party was the BSI Guide, published in March 1986. The first meeting of the NHBC working party was in April. The working party took a practical view of the BSI guidance, and for practical and economic reasons adopted a slightly more relaxed approach to the security requirements for locking hardware which was more in line with earlier research findings on burglary than with the BSI Guide. Since one of the authors had been invited to join the group, it provided an opportunity to introduce some of the ideas which had emerged from our research. The general idea that layout might be as important if not more important than security was accepted by the working party, and the NHBC guidance introduced the notion that autocrime would be reduced if adequate on-curtilage parking was provided. The other innovation in official guidance was the introduction of the idea of a secure private area at the rear of the dwelling and consequent need for bins and meters to be located outside such an area.

The *NHBC guidance on how the security of new homes can be improved* (National House-Building Council, 1986) was published in October 1986, and in February 1987 the Department of the Environment produced an information sheet on layout and security in housing to augment earlier published information associated with a film on housing layout called 'More than Just a Road' (Department of the Enivronment, 1984). Its recommendations seem to be partly influenced by our research and the NHBC working party and other writings on crime and design that had begun to emerge. It is also influenced by the generally accepted social ideas of architecture and planning, with such general exhortations as 'design for a sense of community' – which to us seems like the sort of guidance people give when they have run out of clearly thought-out recommendations. Perhaps the main innovation in these guidelines was the idea of keeping 'the number of road and footpath entrances to a minimum'.

One item that is referred to in this DoE guidance, and to a lesser extent in the BSI Guide, is the idea of avoiding dark corners or hiding places along footpaths to avoid being attacked or robbed. As you will see there is no reference to mugging or violence in the study presented in this book. The truth is that violent attacks on strangers in low-rise housing areas seem very rare. The problem is probably more one of fear in inner city medium- and high-rise estates. The crime data available to us led us to regard violent attacks in public places as too rare to derive any strong recommendations for the housing designer. However, if we did have evidence of more incidents of this kind we would certainly want to consider the matter again. For the moment this requirement has not been demonstrated as sufficiently significant.

About a year after the NHBC guidelines were published, the journal of the House Builders' Federation, *House Builder*, published an article from Professor Alice Coleman which in the words of its title demanded 'More sensitive house-design criteria please!' (Coleman, 1987). In this article Professor

Coleman sets out twelve design features which she considers have proved beneficial in controlling social problems – particularly crime. The first four are designed to encourage surveillance of the street and specify front ground-floor windows, preferably a walk-in bay, and houses facing each other with no projecting features. The next four define a front garden with front and side fences and a gate, which are partly aimed at controlling the behaviour of children. The third group of four specifies houses facing onto quiet through roads with pavements, using corner house designs with windows which face onto both of the intersecting streets, and avoiding back gates and open land at the back.

Having read much of Professor Coleman's work, we have not found any direct empirical evidence for her ideas based on crime data. What seems to be her main justification for these proposals is her belief that the kind of housing built in the 1930s was close to the ideal housing and is believed to be safe from crime and vandalism. We certainly believe that there is some truth in her generalizations, but they do not all seem to be strongly supported by good evidence and some important aspects are omitted. For example, she says nothing about car crime, which is clearly the largest crime problem numerically in housing. She also claims much for the front garden and gates and fences. We certainly have some evidence for a front garden space but the need for front boundary fences and gates

TABLE 12.1 Comparison of security guidelines for low-rise housing

Requirements	BSI	NHBC	DoE	Coleman
1 Moderate locking security	More	Same	nr	nr
2 Facing windows	nr	nr	Less	More*
3 High fences at the sides and rear	nr	Same	Less	Same
4 Front access to a secure yard	nr	Less	nr	Same
5 Access for servicing and deliveries	nr	Less	nr	nr
6 Space at the front	nr	nr	nr	Same
7 On curtilage hardstanding for cars	nr	Same	Less	nr
8 A garage at the side of the house	nr	nr	nr	nr
9 Limit road access	nr	nr	Same	nr
10 Avoid through pedestrian routes	nr	Less	Less	nr
11 Surveillance of access roads	nr	nr	nr	Less
12 Green spaces outside housing areas	nr	nr	nr	nr

*In the original document Coleman has four separate items under this heading. These included having a ground floor window facing the street, preferably with a walk-in bay, no projecting features such as a porch or pram shed, as well as windows facing across the street.

The items are assessed in relation to our own proposals, as specifying 'More', the 'Same', or 'Less' than our requirements (nr indicates no reference is made to our requirements).

is less well supported. In our study some relatively crime free housing had open planned fronts with no low walls or fences. But with this evidence it would be a foolhardy social scientist who would insist on them being included in all new housing. Our views about Coleman's design features are that we agree with most but not all, and that we have included others she has not considered.

The four sets of guidelines referred to above sum up the principal guidance on security in low-rise housing currently available in the UK. We have set out a brief comparison of these in relation to our own findings in *Table 12.1*. The general impression is that already there is some agreement about the features of layout, but we feel justified in claiming to have presented the most complete and well-researched set of requirements so far available.

Relationships with other guidelines for housing design

The recommendations we have made in Chapter 11 do not seem to us to be too difficult to incorporate into current practice. Indeed as will become clearer later in this chapter, many current developments already meet most of these requirements. However, before discussing current practice, it is worth considering how far our proposals agree with or run counter to current guidelines on housing design and layout. In particular, the two published documents which seem to be relevant are the DoE's *Design Bulletin 32: Residential Roads and Footpaths* (Noble, Elvin and Whitaker, 1977) and *A Design Guide for Residential Areas,* first published in 1973 by Essex County Council (Essex County Council, 1983) with a supplement on Highway Standards published in 1980 (Essex

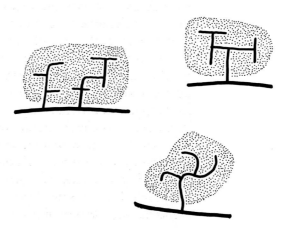

Figure 12.1 Diagrams adapted from the DoE's *Design Bulletin 32: Residential Roads and Footpaths*, illustrating branching cul-de-sac layouts.

Figure 12.2 Diagrams adapted from the DoE's *Design Bulletin 32: Residential Roads and Footpaths*, illustrating through routes in housing areas.

County Council, 1980). This county was so successful in producing its own guidance that it has become an unofficial guide for house design throughout the country and known simply as the 'Essex Guide'.

Design Bulletin 32 provides guidance to ensure safe vehicular movement in residential areas and safe and convenient footpath routes. In so doing, some of the recommendations seem to help the control of crime while others do the opposite. Of the options for planning roads to exclude unwanted traffic and reduce the speed and flow of vehicles in residential areas, there are a number of layouts showing branching cul-de-sac systems which seem to fulfil our Requirement 9 very well (see examples in *Figure 12.1*). However, when the authors accept through routes provided they are longer or more tortuous than the more major routes, as in the diagrams in *Figure 12.2*, then this may be less satisfactory because it allows potential criminals to drive or walk through an area and search for likely targets.

Design Bulletin 32 provides us with more of a problem when it discusses the requirements for footpaths. The main problem is that the *Bulletin* encourages paths to be segregated from the road network. The reason is mainly to keep pedestrian movement away from heavily trafficked routes, but this encourages the pedestrian through routes which we have found increase the risk of crime. It is interesting that there is reference to personal safety on these footpaths by specifying that they should be 'busy, overlooked by dwellings or passing traffic and well-lit after dark', but we doubt if this would make much difference to their contribution to burglary and autocrime as they create opportunities to search for targets and provide ready escape routes. Figures 27 and 28 in the *Bulletin* clearly encourage the introduction of through pedestrian routes which are so common in the Northampton housing built since the *Bulletin* was published (*Figure 12.3*).

The Essex Guide is much more comprehensive in its proposals for housing design and in a number of ways it conflicts with the findings of our research. In an effort to

Figure 12.3 Figures 27 and 28 adapted from the DoE's *Design Bulletin 32: Residential Roads and Footpaths*. These clearly encourage through pedestrian routes and provide easy escape routes.

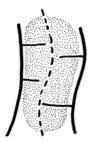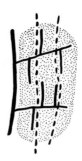

encourage more economic use of land, the Essex Guide discourages the use of front gardens as a waste of space and argues that the problems of privacy can be dealt with quite adequately with narrower windows closer to the footpath, in the manner of our traditional historic towns. The problem for us is that our evidence suggests that there is some value in creating some front semi-private space to protect the front door area and provide supervised car parking. Bringing the building line further forward could make it more difficult to supervise the garage or parking area. The solution often favoured by the authors of the Essex Guide is to recess the parking space with the garage at the side of the house (*Figure 12.4*).

There is no concern shown in the Essex Guide over back gates into gardens of terraced or other housing types. The reason for back fences to be above eye level is to give privacy between houses; security was not an issue when the Guide was drafted. Similarly, there is no requirement for access to the back garden or yard to be through an entrance at the front of the house.

The Essex Guide spells out the idea of segregated footpaths even more clearly than *Design Bulletin 32*. 'Within new housing areas pedestrian movement shall be made convenient, safe and pleasant, by the provision of carefully positioned and well-designed "pedestrian spine routes" and "local access footpaths".'

Two further points also seem to point in the wrong direction. The Essex Guide recognizes what it calls 'Formal Arcadia' in which the layout is dominated by the existing landscape features and where housing is planned in low densities. There is no attempt in these settings to control access to the rear of the houses. The other aspect is that of car parking. The main criterion for parking cars seems to be visual and examples of communal parking spaces and

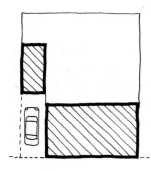

Figure 12.4 Example of a dwelling unit meeting the requirement of the Essex Guide (Source: Essex County Council.)

Figure 12.5 Essex Guide case study on estate layout. (Source: Essex County Council.)

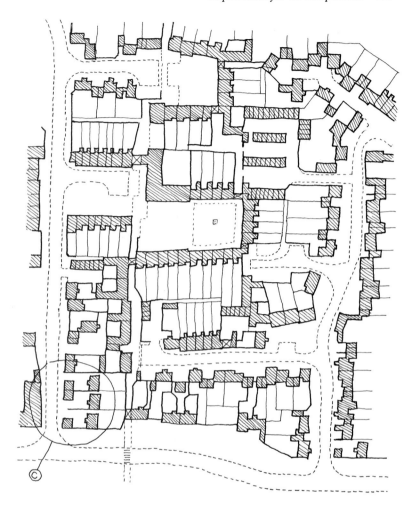

communal garage courts are frequently illustrated in the Guide.

A further demonstration of the difference between the ideas presented by the Essex Guide and the requirements proposed in this book is given in the case study of estate layout presented in the original Essex Guide. *Figure 12.5* reproduces the original recommended alternative layout in a simplified form. If we take our requirements for layout one by one we find the following.

Facing windows
In general this relationship is maintained in this layout. Most houses face others across a street or square, and would provide good front surveillance. However, one house type has a double garage in front of the house, making front surveillance impossible (*Figure 12.5* C).

High fences at the sides and rear

It would seem that all back gardens are intended to be fenced but there is no insistence on full-height walls or fences between gardens.

Front access to a secure yard

This is generally not provided. All houses have back gardens but few have access at the front. Terraces have back alleyways and most other houses are linked and have access to rear gardens only through garages.

Access for servicing and deliveries

It is not possible to judge this aspect of the layout because it would require a much more detailed drawing.

Space at the front

There is little or no semi-private space at the front of the terraced housing in the squares.

On-curtilage hardstanding for cars

Houses with attached garages do have hardstandings on-curtilage, but terraced housing has to rely on communal parking areas and remote garage courts.

Garage at the side of the house

There are some garages in this safe location but for many houses the garages are in garage courts. A number of garages are planned at the far end of the garden.

Limit road access

Although the guide advocates a hierarchical road system which does generally limit road access, the case study does include two major through roads.

Avoid through pedestrian routes

Because of the use of a central pedestrian spine and its connections to each roadway and garage court, this layout has the makings of a rabbit warren. It encourages strangers to wander about and provides a good escape route system.

Surveillance of access roads

It is interesting to see in this example that the road access points are well supervised compared with the pedestrian spine route which is entirely without supervision.

Green spaces outside housing areas

There are several communal green spaces in this layout. Two form part of the pedestrian pathway system with houses facing onto them. These would be attractive to youths and children, and we could imagine that this is where some criminal damage and other nuisance might occur.

In short, we would expect this 'recommended' layout to suffer all kinds of residential crime. It is not wholly bad but in time the housing estate could become a problem area for crime.

Some current housing developments

One of the fortunate outcomes of this research is to find that much of the present-day housing developments already contain many of the recommendations in this book. This is particularly the case in middle and upper-middle income housing currently on offer from the house-building industry. However, problems do exist, particularly in the lower-priced developments where terraced housing and small one- and two-bedroomed houses are included in the development. To illustrate these points, five examples taken from current and recent developments for sale are discussed.

One of the attractive features of current housing for sale is that there are now many well-illustrated brochures being

Figure 12.6 A development of middle-income detached houses which seems to incorporate most of the design characteristics required for a crime free environment.

produced which illustrate both the house types for sale and the layout of the developments. An example of a reasonably successful layout is shown in *Figure 12.6*. This is a middle income development on a single branching cul-de-sac. All the houses are detached, with garages. For the most part, garages are located at the side of the house, although in two plots they are situated at the bottom of the garden. The backs of the houses are all well fenced, and can be provided with side gates opening to the front of the houses as we recommend. The houses themselves generally face houses opposite, and the level of surveillance in all the culs-de-sac and the main access road seems generally good. The only fault which has begun to creep into this layout is the introduction of one or two paths into neighbouring developments. These might encourage some more enterprising burglars, but they do not provide easy through routes. Our general conclusion is that this should be a relatively crime free development.

As houses go up-market, they tend to require larger plots with larger projections such as garage blocks at right angles to the house. The effect of this is to make it more difficult to group houses so that access to the back is properly restricted and at the same time houses face other houses across the street.

The example in *Figure 12.7* shows a medium-sized infill site. The layout designer has clearly done his best to create

Figure 12.7 Mutual surveillance is more difficult to achieve in this development of more up-market detached houses. The footpaths leading out of the area may also cause problems.

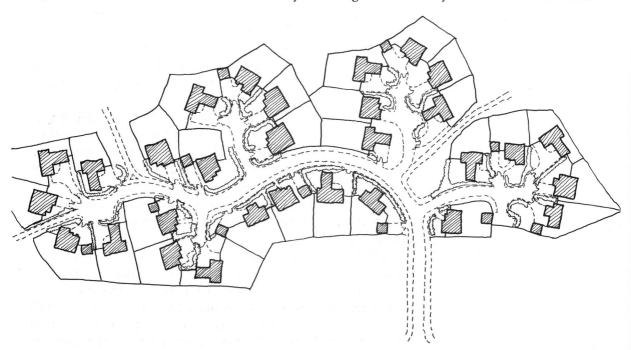

Figure 12.8 The grouping of houses in this development of middle-income housing on an infill site achieves very strong surveillance over the road entrance to the site.

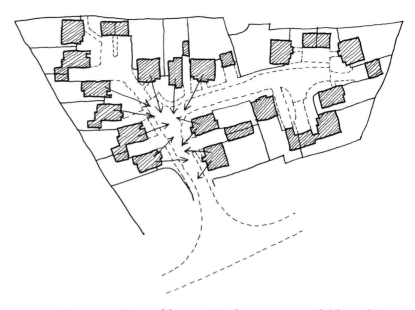

attractive groupings of houses in the spaces available to him, and within each group there is a reasonable amount of mutual surveillance. Because the plots are larger and some have awkward shapes with fronts and sides exposed, the designers have created a waist-high fence or hedge and gates at the front of most properties to give more clearly defined frontages. All back gardens have full-height fences as we have recommended, but there has been no attempt to limit through pedestrian routes. Even in this small development three separate paths lead out to other areas.

Our overall conclusion would be that the design is comparatively secure, but surveillance is not as strong as it could be, and footpaths do encourage through foot-traffic and provide escape routes.

Another example of middle-income infill housing is shown in *Figure 12.8*. Again, it is a single cul-de-sac with detached houses. The particularly good feature about this layout is that on entering the site there are nine houses which overlook the first part of the roadway. We would expect this to provide some discouragement to any intending criminal, and it would seem to us to reinforce quite a strong community feeling of mutual protection.

Modern developments get into more difficulty when small housing units are required. *Figure 12.9* shows part of the development which contains a mixture of detached, semi-detached, and linked or terraced houses with three small blocks of one-bedroomed houses without gardens. It is clear that in the lower cul-de-sac most of our recommended

Figure 12.9 Some of the design requirements are sacrificed to achieve the compactness required in the upper part of this mixed housing development. Problems arise with car parking and the provision of a secure yard accessible from the front of the house.

relationships are retained in a group of detached houses, but in the upper part of the layout a number of important relationships begin to be sacrificed in an attempt to plan more compactly. Where houses are linked together, access to back gardens is either limited to access via the garage or through the house itself. This reduces the value of a secure yard in which a family can leave items such as bicycles and other equipment, and children will tend to leave bicycles unguarded

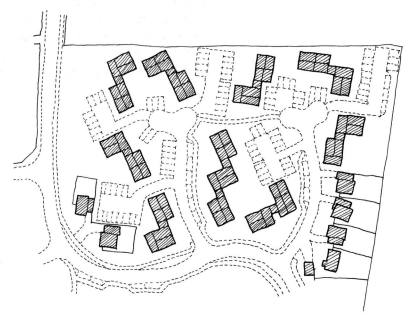

Figure 12.10 A new development of starter homes, showing communal parking away from the houses and no provision of a secure yard.

at the front of the house. However, this does make the rear of the house comparatively secure, and some may prefer this compromise to our recommended requirements.

The problem of car parking for smaller houses where neither driveways nor adjacent garages are provided means that developers rely on communal parking areas. Our research data is not sophisticated enough to know how extensive communal parking has to be before it becomes a real problem. It might not be a serious problem in a development of this scale, particularly where tiny courts have been provided for parking which are overlooked by other houses, but in this case the layout planner has introduced a number of pathways in and out of this group of housing which we would expect to encourage a certain amount of autocrime. Our general view of this particular design is that it is less secure because of the parking and footpath provision, but if it is only a small part of an otherwise secure housing environment we would not expect it to be a serious problem.

The introduction of one-bedroomed houses seems to be becoming a popular idea in the private housing sector for building as starter homes. It is more desirable to have a self-contained house than an apartment, but being planned in blocks of four, or sometimes three, there is no secure yard or garden, and communal parking is the only solution to car parking. *Figure 12.10* illustrates part of a mixed development of houses which shows a very different set of relationships than has been advocated in this book. We have little experience of these developments since few have been occupied for more than a year or so, but they do seem to be vulnerable to all kinds of residential crime, except possibly burglary. It is hard to believe that such developments will remain satisfactory over a long period of time.

13 Finally

What we have tried to do in this book is to define the physical characteristics of low-rise medium-density housing which seem to minimize the risk of crime. In doing so it will have become clear that there are considerable differences in the levels of crime likely to arise from different layout designs. These differences seem to us to be greatly in excess of differences achieved by other kinds of situational variable such as the increased use of locks and alarms. They also seem to achieve greater improvements in crime reduction than any local policing activity, neighbourhood watch programme or any community-based crime-control initiative that we have so far discovered. It is for these reasons we believe that housing layout design is the most effective means of controlling crime in residential areas. Of course this is a long-term policy, but we must remember that the growth of crime has been a long-term process. As we pointed out in the beginning it has taken about forty years for the crime rate to increase eightfold. It was during this period that our urban environment changed a great deal, including the construction of vast amounts of housing in both public and private sectors which do not conform to the recommendations summarized in Chapter 11.

It would be wrong to think that the return to crime levels of the early 1950s is some mad pipe dream. There is every reason to believe, at least as far as housing is concerned, that we can virtually eliminate the problem of residential crime. Already there are many examples of demolition of housing built since 1970 in the UK and there are considerable pressures to build new housing not only on green-field sites but also in urban areas in need of redevelopment.

One complaint that we anticipate from those who will want to criticize these proposals is that the kind of housing being advocated is the sort of suburban housing of the 1960s that the authors of the Essex Guide were so determined to avoid. There is some truth in this in that areas 12 and 16 from our research do represent this kind of 1960s suburban housing and were consistently the least troubled by crime (*Figures 13.1* and *13.2*). However, there is no reason to believe the requirements set out in Chapter 11 prevent attractive housing being designed. There are many recent examples of private

Figure 13.1 Typical view of area 16 – a low crime area.

Figure 13.2 Typical view of area 12 – a low crime area.

developer housing which are both attractive to potential purchasers and which incorporate many if not all the requirements we have specified.

We also recognize that other patterns of design may prove secure in other cultures. Our proposals tend to see the secure threshold or boundary around the house to include the house and a secure yard or garden. In other cultures the boundaries are traditionally different. In North America there is much less of an emphasis on a secure yard, with space around the house offering no significant security. The photographs of traditional housing in Chicago illustrate how the threshold of security to the house does not begin until the stoop or verandah (*Figure 13.3*).

(a)

Figure 13.3(a–c) Traditional
houses in Chicago.

(b)

In warmer European cultures there is more emphasis on
boundary security. Perhaps this is because houses in warmer
climates will have doors and windows left open routinely. It
is not uncommon to see the main security boundary to such
houses at the street entrance with locked gates and facilities
for leaving deliveries, post, etc. Traditional courtyard houses
in India or South America also have an outer boundary as the
principal secure threshold (*Figure 13.4*).

(c)

Figure 13.4 An example of a traditional South American house form (Source: Rapoport (1969).)

Figure 13.5 High security in (a) Hampstead and (b) St John's Wood, London.

(a)

(b)

In up-market housing in the UK there is sometimes the tendency to create an outer secure boundary with high walls, railings and automatic entrance gates (*Figure 13.5*). We also noticed that such an arrangement is common in up-market housing in Hamburg (*Figure 13.6*). The Hamburg examples are interesting because there is a much greater tendency for individual houses to be surrounded by high hedges than similar property in England.

From all this it is clear that there are alternative strategies for domestic security. What seems to be almost unique about the UK suburban housing form is that it combines perimeter security at the rear of the house with a communal social control at the front, derived from implied surveillance by surrounding neighbours. It is not the kind of social relationship in which neighbours are forever running in and out of each other's houses, as might have been the case in nineteenth-century terraced streets. The genius of UK suburban housing is that it combines privacy with just enough mutual surveillance by neighbours to provide a significant social control over potential crime (and no doubt many other aspects of neighbourliness). If perimeter security is extended to include the front of the plot or curtilage, and there is no looking out to the street, we would lose this loose network of social control and we believe our culture would be impoverished. Is it not true that the medium- and high-rise developments of public sector housing designed in the 1960s and 1970s had much the same destructive effect on this network of social control and informal surveillance? Was this not what Oscar Newman (1972) and Jane Jacobs (1962), before him, had been complaining about?

(a)

Figure 13.6(a, b) Perimeter security for private houses in Hamburg.

(b)

References

Baldwin, J. and Bottoms, A. E., 1976, *The Urban Criminal: A Study in Sheffield*, Tavistock Publications, London

Bennett, T. and Wright, R., 1984, *Burglars on Burglary*, Gower, Aldershot

Bottoms, A. E. and Wiles, P., 1988, Crime and housing policy: a framework for crime prevention analysis, in Hope, T. and Shaw, M. (eds.), *Communities and Crime Reduction*, HMSO, London

Brantingham, B. and Brantingham, P., 1984, *Patterns in Crime*, Macmillan, New York

British Standards Institution, 1986, *British Standard Guide for: Security of buildings against crime, Part 1, Dwellings*, London

Coleman, A., 1985, *Utopia on Trial: Vision and Reality in Planned Housing*, Hilary Shipman, London

Coleman, A., 1987, More sensitive house-design criteria please!, *House Builder*, October, 23–26

Coleman, A., 1988, Design improvement of problem estates, in Sime, J. D. (ed.), *Safety in the Built Environment*, E. & F. N. Spon, London

Conklin, J. and Bittner, E., 1973, Burglary in a suburb. *Criminology*, **11**, 206–231

Crime Prevention News, 1987, Issue 3, p. 1, Homes are now more secure, Home Office, London

Crime Prevention News, 1989, Issue 1, (i) p. 6, Big spending on home security, (ii) p. 21, Watch Schemes top 60 000, Home Office, London

Department of the Environment, 1984, *More than just a Road*. Information Sheet No. 13, DoE, London

Essex County Council, 1980, *A Design Guide for Residential Areas: Highway Standards*, Essex

Essex County Council, 1983, *A Design Guide for Residential Areas*, Essex

Farrington, D. P. and Dowds, E. A., 1985, Disentangling criminal behaviour and police reaction, in Farrington, D. P. and Gunn, J. (eds.), *Reactions to Crime: The Public, the Police, Courts, and Prisons*, Wiley, Chichester

Forrester, D., Chatterton, M. and Pease, K., 1988, *The Kirkholt Burglary Prevention Project, Rochdale*, Crime Prevention Unit Paper 13, Home Office, London

Hill, N., 1986, *Prepayment Coin Meters: A Target for Burglary*, Crime Prevention Unit Paper 6, Home Office, London

Home Office, 1981, *Criminal Statistics England and Wales 1980*, HMSO, London

Home Office, 1986a, *Report of the Working Group on Residential Burglary*, HMSO, London

Home Office, 1986b, *A Guide to the Security of Homes*, HMSO, London

Home Office, 1988, *Criminal Statistics England and Wales 1987*, HMSO, London

Hough, M. and Mayhew, P., 1985, *Taking Account of Crime: Key Findings from the 1984 British Crime Survey*. Home Office Research Study No. 85. HMSO, London

Jacobs, J., 1962, *The Death and Life of Great American Cities*, Cape (also published by Penguin in 1964), London

Lipman, A. and Harris, H., 1988, Alice Coleman's dystopia – refusals from 'nowhere', in Teymour, N., Markus, T. A. and Woolley, T. A. (eds.), *Rehumanising Housing*, Butterworths, London

Maguire, M., 1982, *Burglary in a Dwelling*, Heinemann, London

Mayhew, P., Clarke, R. V. G., Stuman, A. and Hough, J. M., 1976, *Crime as Opportunity*, Home Office Research Study No. 34, HMSO, London

National House-Building Council, 1986, *NHBC Guidance on how the Security of New Homes can be Improved*, London

Newman, O., 1972, *Defensible Space: People and Design in the Violent City*. Architectural Press, London

Noble, J., Elvin, K. and Whitaker, R., 1977, *Design Bulletin 32: Residential Roads and Footpaths: Layout Considerations*. HMSO, London

Poyner, B., 1983, *Design against Crime: Beyond Defensible Space*, Butterworths, London

Poyner, B., Helson, P. and Webb, B., 1985, *Layout of Residential Areas and its Influence on Crime*, The Tavistock Institute of Human Relations, London

Poyner, B. and Webb, B., 1987, *Lisson Green Estate, Westminster: Walkway Demolition*, The Tavistock Institute of Human Relations, London

Poyner, B., Webb, B. and Woodall, R., 1986, *Crime Reduction on Housing Estates: An Evaluation of NACRO's Crime Prevention Programme*, The Tavistock Institute of Human Relations, London

Rapoport, A., 1969, *House Form and Culture*, Prentice-Hall, New Jersey

Ravetz, A., 1988, Malaise, design and history, in Teymour, N., Markus, T. A. and Woolley, T. A. (eds.), *Rehumanising Housing*, Butterworths, London

Reppetto, T. A., 1974, *Residential Crime*, Ballinger, Cambridge, Mass.

Riley, D. and Mayhew, P., 1980, *Crime Prevention Publicity: An Assessment*. Home Office Research Study No. 63, HMSO, London

Scarr, H. A., 1973, *Patterns of Burglary*, US Department of Justice, Washington, DC

Southall, D. and Ekblom, P., 1985, *Designing for Car Security: Towards a Crime Free Car*, Crime Prevention Unit Paper 4, Home Office, London

Waller, I. and Okihiro, N., 1978, *Burglary: The Victim and the Public*, University of Toronto Press, Toronto

Walsh, D., 1980, *Break-ins: Burglary from Private Houses*, Constable, London

Wilson, S., 1980, Vandalism and 'defensible space' on London housing estates, in Clarke, R. V. G. and Mayhew, P. (eds.), *Designing out Crime*, HMSO, London

Winchester, S. and Jackson, H., 1982, *Residential Burglary*. Home Office Research Study No. 74, HMSO, London

Index